THE
VOICE

THE
VOICE

HOW WE CAN PARTICIPATE,
HOW WE SHOULD RESPOND

DON NORI, SR.

DESTINY IMAGE® PUBLISHERS, INC.

P.O. Box 310, Shippensburg, PA 17257-0310

"Promoting Inspired Lives"

This book and all other Destiny Image, Revival Press, MercyPlace, Fresh Bread, Destiny Image Fiction, and Treasure House books are available at Christian bookstores and distributors worldwide.

For a U.S. bookstore nearest you, call **1-800-722-6774.**

For more information on foreign distributors, call **717-532-3040.**

Reach us on the Internet: **www.destinyimage.com.**

ISBN 13 TP: 978-0-7684-4197-0

ISBN 13 Ebook: 978-0-7684-8752-7

For Worldwide Distribution, Printed in the U.S.A.

2 3 4 5 6 7 8 / 16 15 14 13

CONTENTS

INTRODUCTION

The Voice has been waiting for a long, long time. Eternity cannot hold the anticipation of His will for what He wants to accomplish in the Earth any longer. His Spirit broods over the Earth, looking, moving, waiting for folk like you and me to simply quiet our souls and give ourselves to the inner preparation of the Holy Spirit. Those who deem themselves ready need not apply. But those who give their lives to Him, for all that He has destined, will find themselves in the middle of His purposes for this planet.

Those who will speak His Voice will speak it with His character as well. His Life will flow through the lives of all who have yielded to Him, regardless of their position, their title, or their ordination. He will be preparing the hearts of the believers and ordaining them according to the work of true Brokenness within. The believers will be recognized by their lives, not just by the words that come from their mouths. Intercessors will not just pray; they will become intercession on behalf of the world. The prophets will not just prophesy, but will become prophetic words. The worshipers will become worship.

As the Presence flows from the Throne within our hearts, we, the Melchizedek of God, are the priesthood of believers. Christ in us, we in Him, move from the Holy Place to the Holy of Holies in our understanding of what Jesus did for us on the Cross and in His mighty, death-destroying resurrection from the dead 2,000 years ago.

People cannot regulate this. They cannot control it. They cannot change what has been set in eternity. God will bring it to its final conclusion. He will use simple folk like you and me who simply believe what He has said and step into His dimension of reality in order to bring His victorious reality into our dimension.

This, then, is what you will read in the pages of this book. Fasten your seat belts. It's going to be a ride. If you will believe, it will change your life forever!

CHAPTER 1

THE LIMP OF JACOB

Brokenness knocked on my door for many years. Patient, compassionate, loving, understanding, faithful Brokenness. God wanted to get my attention, but I was too busy to listen to His Voice. Sure, I wanted to change the world, but after many painful years, Brokenness was finally my friend. At first I wanted to make a peace treaty with her. "You stay there, and I will stay here. You don't bother me, and I won't bother you."

That didn't work. I had no idea what she wanted or who had sent her. She seemed to be more worried about me than I was. It took years, but she taught me that changing myself and changing the world happen simultaneously, and she taught me the importance of hearing the Voice. Now *that* was something totally new to me.

I found Brokenness has been around a long, long time. When Jacob wrestled all night long with the Lord's angel, it was Brokenness that intervened (see Gen. 32). Jacob did prevail, and the hollow of his thigh was thrown out of joint. The Voice said to Jacob, *"Let me go."*

Jacob said, *"I will not let you go unless you bless me."* Brokenness came to Jacob in his suffering and the Lord's mercy. Jacob's name was changed to Israel, and he was given power with God and people. The Lord rewarded Jacob's persistence by blessing him abundantly.

In His gentleness He changes us from self-centered, self-motivated folk to people who genuinely love Union with Him. Union with Him is the goal, and Union is the yearning of our Lord yet today.

Brokenness teaches us what we will never do in ourselves. She teaches us what we would rather not do, what we would rather hoard in ourselves, in our hearts, in our pride. You see, Brokenness gives first, heals first, hopes first, loves first. She intercedes instead of accuses, covers instead of reveals, gathers and does not scatter, builds and does not destroy.

Brokenness is content with God's love and assurance. She does not covet the adulation of mere mortal humans; neither does she demand attention or recognition, as though her gifts are only costume jewelry purchased in the marketplace of religious popularity and emotional fanfare.

Brokenness…she's hard to figure out. In the early days, I had a love-hate relationship with her. Now? Well, now I cannot imagine life without her. But I still shiver when I see her coming.

THE ONLY SAFE PLACE ON EARTH

For one thing, from Brokenness I've learned that the only safe place on Earth or in the spirit realm is to be hidden in Christ. I certainly have many scars that have helped me to understand this. It is a lesson I learned in the trenches and the battlefields of life.

For example, I once thought I was God's gift to humanity as I went from place to place in my efforts to save the world. The reality, though, was that I was more like a bull in a china shop. When I think back on those fleshy efforts, I actually feel sick about them. Nonetheless, God used me, in spite of myself. He loves to use us no matter what our stage of spiritual growth may be.

The more I see the Lord working in my life, the more clarity I find in the conversation John the Baptist had with his disciples:

> *And they came to John and said to him, "Rabbi, He who was with you beyond the Jordan, to whom you have testified, behold, He is baptizing and all are coming to Him." John answered and said, "A man can receive nothing unless it has been given him from heaven. You yourselves are my witnesses that I said, 'I am not the Christ,' but, 'I have been sent ahead of Him.' He who has the bride is the bridegroom; but the friend of the bridegroom, who stands and hears him, rejoices greatly because of the bridegroom's voice. So this joy of mine has been made full. He must increase, but I must decrease"* (John 3:26-30).

John the Baptist understood the work of Brokenness. He rejoiced to know that his preaching was paving the way for the Lord Jesus. His ministry, as ours should be, was to make straight the way of the Lord, to show the way with simplicity and love, to gather, as it were, people to Jesus and His Kingdom here and now. This is what John was doing. As a result, John, as we should, decreased as Jesus increased. If He is not increasing, the appropriate question to ask is "Why?"

John the Baptist realized that we can do nothing on our own. We need the Lord. We can't receive anything unless we get it from Heaven. This is so important for us to realize. John the Baptist knew the meaning of Brokenness. He said, "I will become less important." The theme of our lives should be: "More of Jesus—less of me."

The Voice of One Crying in the Wilderness

John the Baptist was broken before the Lord. This allowed him to become the Voice of God:

> *Now in those days John the Baptist came, preaching in the wilderness of Judea, saying, "Repent, for the kingdom of heaven is at hand." For this is the one referred to by Isaiah the prophet when he said, "THE VOICE OF ONE CRYING IN THE WILDERNESS, 'MAKE READY THE WAY OF THE LORD, MAKE HIS PATHS STRAIGHT!'"* (Matthew 3:1-3).

We are also the Voice of one crying in the wilderness. We are His Voice in this weary land. If we allow His Voice to speak through us, He will increase, and we will decrease. The River of God is never empty; it is flowing from our hearts and out to the world around us. We must let the River of His Voice literally gush forth from deep within our spirits, and then flow out to the spiritual wasteland that is all around us. *"There is a river whose streams make glad the city of God, the holy dwelling places of the Most High"* (Ps. 46:4).

We will learn to view ourselves as simply being the banks of His mighty River, through which the Presence of God flows freely. It is a force that cleanses, purifies, and brings change as it flows. Like water, the Voice of the Lord is all-consuming. It quenches our spiritual thirst and all it touches.

We merely yield to Him, allowing His Voice to rise within us while flowing out from us like a tsunami, so that people will see Him, embrace Him, love Him, want Him, and serve Him. As He increases, we will decrease. We will become more and more a vessel through which His Voice flows to a searching, desperate world.

We will speak His words, not our own. We will be led by Him, flowing where He wants to flow, carrying His gentle, all-consuming love to those who are ready to receive it.

REMEMBER WHERE YOU CAME FROM

Let's not forget where we came from. This gives us a good perspective on ourselves, showing us that we will always desperately need our Lord. When we remember where we came from, we will never think that we have somehow arrived at a place of perfection, because we will know that our personal journey is ongoing.

Sometimes we fail to recall how needy we once were and continue to be now. The whole world is full of desperate needs. Some people even have needs that they don't realize and do not care to admit. Such folk are often unable to express their needs in words. We must remember that where needs abound, grace does much more abound, whether those needs are spiritual, physical, financial, or emotional.

The heart of the Father goes out to needy people, regardless of what their needs may be; but His love does not demand an instant response. Neither does it require religious correctness or doctrinal scrutiny.

Oftentimes, religion accepts or rejects people based on their attire, their speech, their habits, or their worship patterns, if they worship at all. Our God is a gathering God. He gathers people out of the love of His heart. His compassion and desire are to have a family that He knows will be His own. He wants fellowship with the people He created.

Take a look at what happened when Jesus learned about the woman who was taken in adultery. It seems amazing that He required so little of her. After the crowds dispersed, He expressed compassion for her:

> *The scribes and the Pharisees brought a woman caught in adultery, and having set her in the center of the court, they said to Him, "Teacher, this woman has been caught in adultery, in the very act. Now in the Law Moses commanded us to stone such women; what then do You say?" They were saying this, testing Him, so that they might have grounds for accusing Him. But Jesus stooped down and with His finger wrote on the ground. But when they persisted in asking Him, He straightened up, and said to them, "He who is without sin among you, let him be the first to throw a stone at her." Again He stooped down and wrote on the ground. When they heard it, they began to go out one by one, beginning with the older ones, and He was left alone, and the woman, where she was, in the center of the court. Straightening up, Jesus said to her, "Woman, where are they? Did no one condemn you?" She said, "No one, Lord." And Jesus said, "I do not condemn you, either. Go. From now on sin no more"* (John 8:3-11).

Was Jesus condoning sin? Of course not. He was demonstrating that the heart of the Father is far more forgiving than the hearts of most people, including believers. He knew that the Presence carries a convicting power that goes far beyond words of condemnation.

The tender, compassionate Holy Spirit was at work here, as He is in our lives today.

Getting Past Guilt

The world cries for fulfillment. It yearns for a sense of purpose. Most people believe that they were born for a purpose, but they just cannot get past their guilt. Even when they come to Jesus, their leaders make it almost impossible for them to understand that His death and resurrection dealt with their sins—past, present, and future. This lack of forgiveness ties them to their past. It prevents them from walking into the dream God has dreamed for them; it keeps these tender believers from discovering their purpose. Why? Because they are haunted by sin—the sin that has already been paid for by Jesus. Therefore, the world is full of despair and hopeless believers.

Jesus restores, heals, and delivers, and He can do this through us, as well. Let's yield our lives to Him; He can use us to help these believers to discover their purpose in life, know God, and become His Voice to the world.

A Place of Discovery

Brokenness showed me that, instead of arriving at a place of perfection, I have arrived at a place of true discovery. One of those discoveries was the pit of fleshy humanity out of which God has pulled me. Someone said, "The path of discovery is not found in new destinations, but in viewing the familiar through fresh eyes."

Brokenness gave me those fresh eyes so that I can see myself, others, and the Lord from a completely new perspective. Another discovery was that the fleshy stench out of which I came had always been an appalling attraction to me. This was somewhat surprising to me. Without realizing it, it had weakened my resolve and disarmed my faith. I hate to admit these things, but they are true.

There were things in my flesh that I still wanted even though I knew they were a stench in my Father's nostrils. I wanted them, I cried out for them, and sometimes I even gave in to them.

Nonetheless, whenever I smell that fleshy stench, it serves to keep me humble, repentant, small in my own eyes; and it keeps me calling out to God. The apostle Paul always remembered the Cross of Jesus Christ, no matter how many deep revelations he received. As we read his writings, we see how often he remembered who he once was and how respectfully he viewed his own salvation. He found his glory in the Cross of Christ; that is where our glory should be, as well.

Remembering who we once were is essential to Brokenness' vital work in our lives. Our lives before Christ help us to know many things: how we've changed through Him, His power in our lives, how our failures keep us humble, and the importance of decreasing while He increases. This is why I must cling to Brokenness and why Brokenness clings to me, for it is the key to life.

My own memory of the desperation I experienced before Jesus entered my life has become like a magnet that draws me ever closer to the Lord, keeping me broken and penitent before Him. Is this a sign of weakness? No, it keeps me hidden in Christ and helps me to be soft as I listen for the Lord's Voice. It keeps me open to whatever work God wants to do within me and through me. My weakness leads to ever stronger Union with my Creator, who is my everlasting strength.

It is very exciting to discover that God is building this kind of resolve in people all over the world. He wants His will to be done in people's lives; there is no doubt about that. His desire to see this happen is far greater than our desire to do it. If we remain open, however, He will teach us, mold us, and prepare us to be all that His heart wants us to be. In this way, His will shall be accomplished.

We can be the Voice that releases people to pursue and find the dream and purpose God has for them. Sometimes, though, believers turn people away from their purpose by presenting God in ways that are doctrinally narrow, not showing the clear love and forgiveness of Jesus.

We must be His arm extended, reaching out to the oppressed. We must be His Voice amplified, speaking to the needs of people everywhere in loud and clear tones that will draw them to Him.

WHAT IS IMPORTANT TO GOD?

Some may think that filling up their churches is the most important thing, regardless of how it is done. Others may think that filling up Heaven is first and foremost in God's heart. Releasing God's plan for people will open them to Heaven. The Western version of Christianity focuses on Heaven. Jesus, on the other hand, was focused on the here-and-now. It is time for us to be more like Jesus.

Notice how Jesus taught the disciples to pray:

> *Pray, then, in this way: "Our Father who is in heaven, hallowed be Your name. Your kingdom come. Your will be done, on earth as it is in heaven. Give us this day our daily bread. And forgive us our debts, as we also have forgiven our debtors. And do not lead us into temptation, but deliver us from evil. [For Yours is the kingdom and the power and the glory forever. Amen]"* (Matthew 6:9-13).

As we learn to yield to the Lord within, He will reeducate us. He will show us His purposes in the Earth and His purposes for us. It is essential that we permit Him to change the way we think. The flow of His Presence within us depends upon this. He will be all that we need. As someone has said, "If all we have is God, He is all that we need."

Our Western understanding of religion was ingrained within us as a system that would take us from generation to generation. The Kingdom of God needed to go on, but the Kingdom is Christ-centered, and it is present-tense focused. This Kingdom is led by the King of kings, the great I AM, and the Lord of lords who rules from the timelessness of eternity, where there is no yesterday or tomorrow—only *now*.

Yes, God's Kingdom is coming, God's Kingdom has come, but most importantly, it is here right now, and it is found within us.

> *He again fixes a certain day, "Today," saying through David after so long a time just as has been said before, "TODAY IF YOU HEAR HIS VOICE, DO NOT HARDEN YOUR HEARTS"* (Hebrews 4:7).

Listen for God's Voice today, and follow what He tells you. You will not regret it.

THE KINGDOM OF GOD

The Kingdom of God is vastly different from what we have been led to believe. We must remain open, pliable, willing, and yielded in order to let the Voice rise within us and flow out from us. As we learn to hear His Voice, the Voice will teach us about who He is. We will learn to view things the way He views them.

*Many nations will come and say, "Come and let us go up to the mountain of the L*ORD *and to the house of the God of Jacob, that He may teach us about His ways and that we may walk in His paths." For from Zion will go forth the law, even the word of the L*ORD *from Jerusalem* (Micah 4:2).

Jesus said:

Come to Me, all who are weary and heavy-laden, and I will give you rest. Take My yoke upon you and learn from Me, for I am gentle and humble in heart, and YOU WILL FIND REST FOR YOUR SOULS. *For My yoke is easy and My burden is light* (Matthew 11:28-30).

But an hour is coming, and now is, when the true worshipers will worship the Father in spirit and truth; for such people the Father seeks to be His worshipers (John 4:23).

These three passages give us a greater understanding of Brokenness and Union with God. God is teaching us His ways so that we would walk in His paths. He has provided rest for us and has shown us the way. He wants us to worship Him in the true way and with the right spirit.

His Kingdom will come as we are taught by the Voice.

THE OUTWARD JOURNEY

True Union is not ultimately an inward journey. Instead, it causes you to look outward. Union helps you to understand your Oneness with the Lord. When this Union is cultivated, you will see as He sees, love as He loves, and gather as He gathers.

How does this happen? It happens when your understanding of the process is changed. You know that He is taking care of your needs, desires, and pain. As a result, your focus no longer needs to be upon yourself. The Presence then flows from you to the world. You become driven in the same way He is driven—by His love, to meet the needs of those around you.

Brokenness leads you to discover the River of His Presence within and, ultimately, Union with God. Your discernment, your ministry, your intercession for those who need His Life becomes effective and powerful. Through you, God touches them, both within the Church Jesus is building and in the world outside.

Your journey is now His journey—to a world full of suffering and in great need of redemption. As you carry the Voice to others—your family, your neighborhood, your school, your city, and the nations of the world—you are buttressed by the knowledge that you are yielded to Him, you have given yourself to Him, and you are experiencing the wonderful blessing of Union with Him and the flow of the River of His Presence emanating from you. His Voice is being articulated through you!

His passion drives you. The more you yield yourself to Him, the more you find yourself responding to things that you used to think were impossible. You begin doing things you never thought you would be able to do, and you begin to say things you never expected to say. You are no longer confined by a religious box or a denominational code. You have learned to respond to the Lord alone. This is true freedom.

Life takes on a whole new meaning when these things are in place. The Lord is on the inside, showing you what needs to be addressed on the outside. The more you see and learn, the more you want to give. This happens because you now see the world in the way He sees it. You have been broken with tears of intercession and a heart that wants to gather. You can now hear His Voice speaking to you.

This is the heart—the very life—of intercession, and the result of Union with God. If you yearn for Him in all His fullness, an exciting life awaits you. Union is enjoyed by those who want to fully experience His Presence. Brokenness will lead you to be aware of the Union that is growing within. Union will lead you to intercession.

My prayer is seldom for me, but is always through me toward others. I see, I feel, I sense need and cannot help but pray for those I see. It is a way of life. His Life flows through me, not to me. He is taking care of me.

> *...I know whom I have believed and I am convinced that He is able to guard what I have entrusted to Him until that day* (2 Timothy 1:12).

> *Consider the lilies, how they grow: they neither toil nor spin; but I tell you, not even Solomon in all his glory clothed himself like one of these. But if God so clothes the grass in the field, which is alive today and tomorrow is thrown into the furnace, how much more will He clothe you? You men of little faith! And do not seek what you will eat and what you will drink, and do not keep worrying. For all these things the nations of the world eagerly seek; but your Father knows that you need these things. But seek His kingdom, and these things will be added to you* (Luke 12:27-31).

Life with the River of His Presence flowing through you changes everything, especially how you think, and how you believe. Knowing that you are completely cared for turns your attention outward, and you discover and respond to the needs of those around you.

BROKENNESS PERMITS NO PRIDE

How do we live in brokenness without pride? Is it even possible for a human being to do so? This is so important to understand. Religious people (in their pride) have done a lot of damage. They have injured many who were seeking God by giving them the wrong kind of direction. This causes many of us to feel like running away from anything that resembles faith.

If we do run, it should be in the direction of the genuine, heartfelt, Christ-planted, God-born realities of our authentic spiritual life. All too often, people run in the opposite direction; but the flow of His Life is the real thing.

The religious imposters who use you for their own gain are the ones to run from. Their words seem real because you can hear them with your natural ears and see them with your natural eyes. I have experienced them too many times myself. I have learned to rest in the River of His Presence, the true Reality of Life. He is the true hope of the world, my true hope. Their words mean nothing. I can only rest in Him. There is no other place to go, for only He has the words of eternity.

We must not take the concept of God's Life flowing from deep within as a light matter. His Life was purchased at a tremendously exorbitant price for you and me so we would be His instruments— the instruments of His purpose—in these last days. Never forget that you were saved for His purposes. The blessings we enjoy are the result of being called to His purposes.

Our greatest fellowship is with the Lord who dwells within us. Distinguishing Him from the other things we love could well be considered the chore of a lifetime. But without a doubt, it is a chore that the Spirit of God can help us discern.

Our religious activities, our deeply human voices that sound spiritual, but are nothing more than our lustful, private desires disguising themselves as spiritual voices, are not easily discerned. That is where we learn to rest in the work of the Holy Spirit within. He will help us in the challenging art of discerning the genuine Voice of the Lord.

THE KEY IS HUMILITY

You will hear me say this again and again throughout this book. Brokenness will lead you to discover the River of His Presence within and, ultimately, Union with God. This Union will draw you to other people who will need your discernment so that your intercession for them will be effective and powerful. In this way, God will touch the needy, both within the Church Jesus is building and in the world around you.

Incidentally, meekness is not a form of weakness. It is strength that has been refined through Brokenness. However, Brokenness does not mean that one sacrifices what God is doing to appease our fears for doing what God is saying to do, for in so doing, he or she returns to the lifeless works of people and religion. This must never be.

GOD IS RISING!

I have no desire to bow to the intellectuals, the theologians, or anyone who seeks conformity or denies truth for the sake of the established order of things. Such people disregard the experiences of others for the sake of their half-truths, old theories, and broken systems. These folk are stuck in the patterns that others established for them, the traditions of people, not the ways of God. They are dogmatic and inflexible.

Those who have seen the unseen and have questioned the status quo must continue to let their voices be heard. They must remember that they are not alone. They may not even be in the minority.

An explosion of spiritual hunger is taking place in our times. It is not a class thing, a racial thing, an age thing, or an ethnic thing. What is happening today transcends all these human barriers. God's work in the hearts of humanity even transcends what we have been told to believe as well as think is right. The hunger of our times goes beyond the thoughts and greed of humankind. It rises above all human fear, every personal lust for power and fame. God *is* rising, and all His enemies are being scattered.

Many think the enemies of God are socialism, atheism, political correctness, evolution, and so forth. There is another subset of enemies, however; these are harbored in the hearts of believers and unbelievers alike. These "hidden" enemies include hate, fear, envy, rebellion against God, religious self-assurance, self-righteousness, self-centeredness, pride, anger, and all kinds of lust.

These enemies, as long as they remain unconfessed to the Lord, hide within those of us who call upon Him. It is far easier to recount the cultural enemies of our Lord Jesus than it is to understand that we actually harbor the deepest enemies of His will within ourselves.

The outward enemies that are part of the social ills of our society have no standing when the hearts of those who call Jesus "Lord" actually allow Him to live His Life through them.

The rising of the Lord Jesus will scatter all the enemies of God, even the ones who live in us. We must be ready for this, allowing the

Lord to expose these things in us and being willing to confess their existence in our lives.

How can we expect to raise and carry the banner of truth around the world if we cannot even do so within ourselves? This is not to say that we should strive to be perfect, or that a one-time confession and repentance will end the struggle. I am painfully aware of my own shortcomings and spend ample time in prayer and repentance as a result of them. I do not hide them, make excuses for them, or try to convince myself that these enemies within are not really enemies. I confess them, repent of them, and take full responsibility before God for their existence in me. Then I ask the Lord for the strength to bring their influence in my life to an end.

The process is very much like taking an antibiotic for an infection. One dose rarely does the trick; but a daily regimen of the medication will ultimately kill the infection. Daily prayer and repentance will also rid our lives of the enemies within. This is how it should be. True disciples of Jesus allow and welcome the Holy Spirit to police their souls. He deeply wants us to come into Union with Him.

This humble lifestyle of allowing Brokenness to monitor us keeps us in constant communication with the Voice of the Lord, who will gently tell us the good, the bad, and the ugly about our lives, in a manner that is filled with His mercy and grace. Our relationship with Jesus keeps us in check with Him, as He shows us things we have never seen before. This is true friendship with God.

God is rising, and the people of God are being stirred by a Love that cannot be contained, restrained, constrained, or eliminated by the church system that has little to do with the Church that Jesus is building. The system thought it had the Holy Spirit contained, but how wrong the system was to think that. Historically, as the Holy Spirit moved in the Earth, the system was able to suck this new life into the "black hole" of lifeless, lightless, and worthless religion.

All to Jesus I surrender,
Humbly at His feet I bow,
Worldly pleasures all forsaken,
Take me, Jesus, take me now.[1]

Oh, Brokenness, how thankful I am to you, because you have opened the door to Union with God, which is the main topic of my next chapter.

Endnote

1. Judson W. Van DeVenter, "I Surrender All" (1896).

CHAPTER 2

UNION—THE RESTFUL LAUNCH

U nion with God. The mystics sought it diligently. There was a passion, a drive, a fire within them that would not be satisfied without Union. Their search became a pattern for those who were to follow, those who carried the same undying fire of heart. It is no wonder that their reflections on Union have been the source of much study and meditation over the years. Their words have become a launching pad, so to speak, for many who will discover what follows where their journeys concluded.

Brokenness teaches us as we continue on the journey. Responding to the Presence of the Lord Jesus deep within, we will discover the Union with God that will change our relationship with Him forever. For me, my journey has uncovered some of the most remarkable thoughts about Him. They have revolutionized nearly everything I thought I knew about Him. They have brought me closer to Him with more assurance, more confidence, more peace than ever before. I am more confident that I am His. He is in me forever. He will take me wherever He wants me. I do not need to push, force, scheme, or in any way show myself as better than another. He will simply put me where He wants me to be, so I can do what He wants me to do. After all, He is in me. Isn't that enough?

I was a very young man when He first tried to show me this. I started writing books. Although I owned an international publishing company, I did not want to market them as I did other books. I simply listed them for sale. When my sons came into the business, they began to market, advertise, and sell them. I could not push myself forward. Personally, I believed I had an unfair advantage; I owned the company. On the other hand, my sons saw my material as needed in the marketplace and so began to promote my teaching.

Union is a restful state of living, of being. The believer rests in Him. He does what He wants through the believer; the world changes.

GENUINE HEARTS

God loves a genuine heart. He will always shower His grace upon anyone who has opened his heart to Him. Indeed, He will open doors for all who have yielded to the River of His Presence to flow freely through them.

He knows His Presence will also bring about personal change and inner transformation within your life as a much needed by-product of your softness of heart toward the Lord Jesus. As He draws you to Himself, you will change your world, but that change will be the result of a change in your life. He will often take you to those you need to forgive or who need to forgive you. Such inner change releases your heart to love and care for the world around you in ways you cannot imagine until it actually happens.

Brother Lawrence wrote,

> This union [with God] is not a mere fleeting emotion,
> such as would prompt a passing cry like, 'My God, I
> love Thee with my heart's full strength.' It is, instead,

a state of soul—if I can but find words—that is deeply spiritual and yet very simple, which fills us with a joy that is undisturbed, and with a love that is very humble and reverent.[1]

Such Union is an experience for all who will rest in Him.

A YEARNING FROM DEEP WITHIN

What is man that You take thought of him, and the son of man that You care for him? Yet You have made him a little lower than God, and You crown him with glory and majesty! (Psalms 8:4-5).

The created being is desperately searching for Union with its Creator. That, however, is only half of the story. God is infinitely more interested in us than we are in Him! We love Him, but we carry around such a sense of guilt and shame that we cannot seem to shake. We are restricted by our past "stuff" in our ability to love Him openly and freely. This also causes us to sometimes think that God isn't really interested in us at all. We must learn how to deal with and discard the baggage that we have brought into our relationship with God.

I wonder how many marriages never happen because someone is loved from a distance, thinking that true love could never happen. With our Lord, though, it is far more than just a case of true love; it is Union, oneness, the synchronous movement of thought, love, and life in time and space, where the River of His Life engulfs us and transforms us into a species that has never been seen on this planet before.

There is no doubt that God is yearning for those through whom He can express His Love and Presence. The average church leaders see themselves as cowhands trying to herd animals who don't have a clue, from one watering hole to another, keeping them from the wolves, the cliffs, the thieves, and each other. These leaders don't understand the power of His love or of His mighty compassion. They often do not understand His Presence to gather, heal, restore, and protect His own. God's people are more than they are given credit for. The Believers' Priesthood, the Holy Nation, if taught and released into their inheritance, is a force that the world has not seen and the gates of hell have no power to withstand.

This is more essential than most people understand, and it is certainly not for the faint of heart. God's Spirit flows through mere folk like you and me, and this makes His Church a thing of incredible love, beauty, power, and effectiveness. Her power is not to be messed with for her resolve is formidable indeed. This is truly the Church Jesus is building.

It is the believer's Union with God that brings about the beauty that the world wants and needs to see. The world seldom sees it, because true Union is so uncommon.

Likewise, a happy marriage is a beautiful thing to see. A happy couple with happy children sows happiness wherever they go. It is simply a natural outflow of who they are. They leave this atmosphere of joy and contentment as their mark. They don't write manuals on how to be happy, and they don't even talk about their strategies for happiness. They are just being themselves. Who they are radiates from them and makes others thirsty for the same thing.

Such is also the case with our Union with God. Our Union with Him is visible. It is natural to us, but unnaturally visible to others. When others are around a person who has true Union with God, they feel something that is different and unique. They know there is something unusual in the air that makes them want to be around the people who know true Union.

In the lives of these people, the life of God is more memorable than the witness of any booklet or tract; and it is certainly more lasting. It stirs their hearts within and often ignites an inner fire that causes them to fall hopelessly in love with their Creator. It puts them on a journey that will change their lives forever.

INTERCESSION—A NATURAL PART OF UNION

Most people think that intercession is simply praying for someone else, but it is far more than that.

There is a portal through which God's will flows. When Christ rises through us to draw His unlimited, timeless dimension into our limited dimension of time and space, that portal opens up. It is within the Most Holy Place, our hearts, where He has taken up permanent residence. He sits upon His Throne, in the throne room that is within.

His Presence surges through our hearts, a mighty River carrying His Voice and will into our dimension. Sometimes we don't recognize it, but that does not mean we are free from the responsibility to allow the Presence to bring needed intercession through our hearts.

Many times the Lord uses us even though we do not understand what may be happening both within and without. It reminds me of the processes involved with breathing. We take air in, and that air sets off a chain of events we may never comprehend. This must happen in spite of our ignorance of the processes that are taking place. These processes keep us alive.

The more we understand the spiritual processes that take place through intercession, the more we will be able to yield to those processes and become willing participants in God's purpose for us. That, of course, is the ultimate goal.

It is the anticipation of being a part of His plan that drives me to want to yield to Him as much as my fleshy desires will allow. That's the crux of the matter. It is sometimes a struggle to find that place. I confess that no matter how much I would like to yield to Him, my fleshy humanity puts up a strong resistance to His drawing power.

I realize that I am not alone in this, for every earnest seeker has to go through it. It's a part of the process of spiritual growth. Paul wrote:

> *No temptation has overtaken you but such as is common to man; and God is faithful, who will not allow you to be tempted beyond what you are able, but with the temptation will provide the way of escape also, so that you will be able to endure it* (1 Corinthians 10:13).

The only solution to the problem is to repent of the resistance that my flesh puts forth and then to go on, giving myself to the Lord all over again. It is only through the process of repentance that I learn the discipline of keeping my mind aware of the Presence that flows through me like a mighty River.

This is ultimately not difficult. It is like being aware of your children on a playground as you carry on a conversation. You are always conscious of them. You know where they are and what they are doing, even though some of your attention is focused elsewhere.

DRAWING FROM HIS PRESENCE

God takes up His residence within us. He finds His home in mortal people. This is how He reaches others. This is how we are able to enter into the other-dimensional no-man's land beyond what we are able to perceive with our physical senses.

It is here—in the Most Holy Place within us—that the Holy Spirit looks for all that is Him, all that is Spirit, in order to draw it to Himself. He pulls all this into time and space, where it is first introduced to our five senses and our emotions, and He expands it to include everything and everyone around us.

This awareness arises in our hearts, flowing into our senses. During these times, God is using us. We are able to realize more fully than ever before that He dwells within us—permanently. What a glorious realization this is!

Now we are ready to draw from His Presence in spite of what we may have been taught through the years. His will, His Kingdom, and the "stuff" of eternity flow through us into time and space for the specific purposes He has in mind.

The Ark of the Covenant is a type of our hearts and the indwelling Christ. The pulsating Presence that at one time dwelt between the wings of the cherubim is actually Christ dwelling within us, within the Most Holy Place, which is our hearts. The indwelling Christ is the center, the focus, the *everything*.

The cherubim that figuratively guarded the glowing Presence on the Ark actually guard the Presence in us. This is a real-time activity in us and around us, a point of dimensional intersection where time and space meet eternity. This phenomenal truth, seen in the Ark of the Covenant for thousands of years, is a reality within you and me today.

The more I focus on this reality, the more I am able to resist the draw of outward distractions. I am no longer interested in things that keep some folk running from meeting to meeting. Such things are manifestations of fleshy Christianity. I want nothing to do with those things any longer. I have no desire to go to a meeting to be entertained. I want to experience the fullness of the Presence of God—or at least as much as I can handle! This I can do no matter where I am or who I'm with. He lives within. The Father is seated within on the Throne of my heart, the Most Holy Place. His Son is seated next to Him. This confluence of dimensions occurs within me and is guarded by angelic beings. What more can I even want?

> *But to which of the angels has He ever said, "SIT AT MY RIGHT HAND, UNTIL I MAKE YOUR ENEMIES A FOOTSTOOL FOR YOUR FEET"? Are they not all ministering spirits, sent out to render service for the sake of those who will inherit salvation?* (Hebrews 1:13-14).

I don't want to be a "spectator Christian" any longer. I want to be a participant in what God is doing. I want to learn to flow with Him.

The greatest miracles of our day are not occurring in the Middle East or in Washington, D.C. They are not happening in great conventions, meetings, or conferences. The greatest miracles are occurring in your heart and mine. It is here, if we are attuned to it, that the fullness of God rises to accomplish His will through us. Therefore, I'm not just sitting around waiting for the Rapture or hoping to be slain in the Spirit or to be coated with gold dust. I'm not waiting for a gold tooth to appear in my mouth, though I could use some. If something spectacular is to occur, I want it to occur within my heart or within my family. Let something happen in those realms that will be of permanent benefit to the Kingdom of God and the Body of Christ—the Church that Jesus is building.

I want to hear the Voice of God speaking to me. *"The voice of the LORD is powerful, the voice of the LORD is majestic"* (Ps. 29:4).

CHRIST-CENTERED LIFESTYLE

About a million years ago, before I understood how much Jesus loved me, I remember how students on my college campus were going around announcing that Jesus would return in five years. I remember how they said that if you didn't believe this, Jesus would leave you behind in the Rapture.

There were others who believed that the Ark had been found in Jerusalem. It didn't take me too terribly long to realize that all these hyped-up ideas were actually spiritual hula-hoops—fads that kept bored Christians running from one place and idea to the next. They kept us excited, but distracted.

It was then that I began to realize that the most important thing was keeping the centrality of Jesus within my heart. That is what would be of permanent benefit to the Kingdom of God and the Church Jesus is building. I wanted Him to increase while I decreased. I wanted Him to be lifted up by my actions, words, and thoughts. A Christ-centered lifestyle keeps my life on course.

> *"For My thoughts are not your thoughts, nor are your ways My ways," declares the LORD. "For as the heavens are higher than the earth, so are My ways higher than your ways, and My thoughts than your thoughts"* (Isaiah 55:8-9).

THE MIND OF CHRIST

Union with God allows our thoughts to line up with His, and His thoughts to become ours. Our minds are renewed, and we begin to see everything from a fresh perspective.

Oswald Chambers wrote,

> Beware of becoming careless over the small details of life and saying, "Oh, that will have to do for now."

Whatever it may be, God will point it out with persistence until we become entirely His.[2]

God wants Union with us to that extent, so much so, in fact, that He will not let us go until we enter in.

The more we appreciate the incredible magnitude of God and His desire to use us, the happier we will become. As for me, it has truly become exciting to just go along for the exhilarating ride. Really! There is nothing more profound than the realization that God wants to involve humanity in His work for this planet.

So I want to yield to Him insofar as I am able to yield. I want to see more, participate more, love more. His love is so amazing, overwhelming, overflowing, and overpowering. I love His love. I love to share it wherever I go. The more I yield to His Voice, His Presence, and His Love, the more I see things changing within me and around me. His love engulfs my will. When this happens, I see afresh that His plan always trumps anything I could ever want. Everything pales to insignificance in the light of His desires for me.

THE CONFLICT

We cannot stuff our needs and desires into His plan and expect good results. We must not try to put our earthly passions upon the Lord. I've tried doing these things, and in the process, I've learned a great deal about who God is and what He wants from me. He wants our will to conform to His, not the other way around.

It seemed as if I was always trying to convince someone (maybe myself, maybe God, maybe others) that my mission was at the center of God's heart. The fact is that it seldom was. It was not at the center of His heart; it was at the center of mine.

Nonetheless, I succeeded in convincing some that what I was doing was all God's idea. Therefore, they would follow me. I thought this meant that they would eventually follow God as well. Of course, for that to happen, I had to convince God that my plans were right; I had to "help Him" to see that my passion was very important.

It's scary to realize it, but people will follow anyone who delivers a passionate message, even if it is a fleshy one. We've seen this happen over and over again—the blind leading the blind and both falling into a deep ditch!

My miserable failures led me to repentance before both God and people. It was not easy for me, and it was certainly no fun to do, but I did it. I repented to God and people again and again. Thank God for His love and for the love of the brethren.

I have learned that the way to truly work with God, to truly agree with His work within, is to simply let Him have His way without trying to second-guess Him. Once the River of His Presence begins to flow through you, He is the One who is on a mission. Don't bother trying to figure it out, because you will get into trouble if you do. Sooner or later, you will endeavor to squeeze in your own passion, your own mission, and your own ministry.

It's a bit of a cliché, but we must remember it's not about us. It's all about what God wants to do through us, in us, and in spite of us.

It's not about expanding your own kingdom either; it's about expanding His. Remember this: God is trying to use you as a true intercessor so He can meet real needs. He is the great need-supplier, and He loves to bless.

Thomas à Kempis wrote:

> Speak, Lord, for Your servant hears. I am Your servant; give me understanding, that I may know Your testimonies. Incline my heart to the Words of Your

mouth: let your Words descend like the dew…You who are the inspirer and enlightener of all the prophets, speak to me—for You alone without them can perfectly instruct me, but without You they can do nothing…Speak, therefore, Lord, for Your servant hears, for You have the words of eternal life. Speak to me so that my soul, however imperfect, will be comforted, my life will be amended, and You will be praised, glorified, and honored forever.[3]

Yes, the Voice of God speaks to true intercessors, but what is a true intercessor? Let's learn more about intercession in the next chapter.

Endnotes

1. Brother Lawrence, *The Practice of the Presence of God* (Alachua, FL: Bridge-Logos, 1999), 137.

2. Oswald Chambers, *My Utmost for His Highest—An Updated Version in Today's Language* (1992), quoted in *God's Treasury of Virtues* (Tulsa, OK: Honor Books, 1995), 427.

3. Thomas à Kempis, *The Imitation of Christ* (Alachua, FL: Bridge-Logos, 1999), 118-119.

CHAPTER 3

THE VOICE
TEACHES US TO PRAY

T rue intercessors are a strange lot. You can't tell them to pray. You can't pay them to pray. You can't follow their line of reason when they do pray. You can't tell them how to pray, how long to pray, or even who to pray for. For they are not directed by people; they are led by the Voice within.

Yes, true intercessors are a strange lot. They simply walk into a situation, a church, a family, a company, a house meeting, a mall. True intercessors perceive what others don't perceive, feel what others don't feel. They see through what others can't imagine. They hear sounds in a silent room and silence at a child's birthday party. For sure, true intercessors are a very strange lot.

They have no personal agenda. They are builders of a Kingdom not of this Earth, and they can smell the sweat of humanity's work a mile away. Their allegiance is centered toward a Kingdom not their own. They are vessels in the hands of their Master. They understand and embrace the work of Brokenness in their hearts.

But they can become disillusioned and depressed easily, for their prophetic vision sees miles ahead of the realities of times and space. Their lives need to be embraced by those who understand their work and love their calling. Their work is not their hobby. They are engulfed in a lifestyle of divine Brokenness, divine yieldedness, divine knowing. Yet, to see them on the street, they are like anyone else—working, shopping, moms, dads, grandparents. They live their lives like everyone else, but for the inner flow of the River of His Presence, to which they have given themselves.

THEY SOMETIMES WALK ALONE

True intercessors don't take prayer requests. To the casual prayer warrior who storms Heaven, this may seem strange, even unkind. But intercessors do not respond to the needs of people; they respond to the will of God and to the River of His Presence flowing from deep within. Intercessors cannot simply agree to pray from a prayer list. Often, the Presence will cause intercessors to pray specific prayers for situations or people from a list, but they pray according to how the Lord is leading, even if it is different from how they were asked to pray.

Remember, a prayer warrior may storm Heaven according to a request, but an intercessor is careful to respond to God. If there is no leading, there is no intercession. There is only one allegiance, to God alone. Personal desires have no place counseling God. There is only His way. There is never "my" way.

Intercessors wait for His heart, for their praying is set by God Himself. He tells them when to pray, what to pray, how to pray, and who to pray for.

Certainly, they can go to the Lord on behalf of an individual, event, or situation, but it is only the Lord who can turn simple prayer into true intercession.

BABBLE OR UNDERSTANDING?

But all of this appears to be selfish babble to the one who does not understand that God has a sacred mission of His own. We have no idea of the eternal intelligence, passionate love, and infinite determination that drive the heart of God as He flows so patiently through the hearts of folk like you and me. He is determined to do His will, and accomplish His plan for us on this little sphere in the vastness of the universe.

Yielding to His Voice is all about Him. For sure, we are cared for in the process, but our fulfillment is not the focus or the goal; yielding to Him is the only goal. The Voice has much to say; as we hear, feel, and respond to the Voice, Heaven and Earth are forever changed. Of this, there is certainly no doubt. The key is to always pray what He wants us to pray, nothing more.

TRUE BROKENNESS—A PREREQUISITE

True discernment, true intercession, and true utterance require true Brokenness as a prerequisite to Union with God and spiritual breakthroughs. The key word here is *true*, for God cannot work with anything that is phony.

When Jesus went to the Pool of Bethesda, He found several sick people and five porches there:

In these lay a multitude of those who were sick, blind, lame, and withered, [waiting for the moving of the waters; for an angel of the Lord went down at certain seasons into the pool and stirred up the water; whoever then first, after the stirring up of the water, stepped in was made well from whatever disease with which he was afflicted.] A man was there who had been ill for thirty-eight years. When Jesus saw him lying there, and knew that he had already been a long time in that condition, He said to him, "Do you wish to get well?" The sick man answered Him, "Sir, I have no man to put me into the pool when the water is stirred up, but while I am coming, another steps down before me." Jesus said to him, "Get up, pick up your pallet and walk." Immediately the man became well, and picked up his pallet and began to walk. Now it was the Sabbath on that day (John 5:3-9).

Notice that Jesus healed only one person and left the rest in their sickness and pain. What person with the gift of healing would do the same today? I think not many. Wouldn't most endeavor to minister to everyone in need? They would have prayer lines and lay their hands on everyone.

Jesus did only what the Father told Him to do. Jesus said:

Therefore Jesus answered and was saying to them, "Truly, truly, I say to you, the Son can do nothing of Himself, unless it is something He sees the Father doing; for whatever the Father does, these things the Son also does in like manner. For the Father loves the Son, and shows Him all things that He Himself is doing..." (John 5:19-20).

In most services today, the pattern is to pray for everyone in the hopes that some will get healed. Then we make excuses for the rest. Jesus, on the other hand, discerned who to pray for, knew they would be healed, and then sent them on their way. He was always moved by compassion, not by any potential monetary offering, a video camera, or His own ego.

He was always moved by His Father's will. We should do exactly the same if we are to be true intercessors. It did not matter to Jesus what the other folk would say about the fact that He only touched one person. Today, if a visiting ministry prayed for only one person, it would be most scandalous! The minister's offering would be lower and future invitations to minister might even decrease. *Better to do what the folk expect rather than what the Father wants. No one would ever know*—except, of course, the minister and the Father—and Brokenness.

INTERCESSION MUST COME FROM WITHIN

True intercession rises from within, where God's wisdom also rises. As the Presence rises in our hearts, His spiritual wisdom replaces all the human wisdom we accumulate through years of training and experiences. Human counsel sometimes has its place, but when true intercession is flowing and the wisdom of God is present, human wisdom can never direct our intercession. I have found that even my own experience cannot be trusted as God moves in ways that I have not seen, even though I have been praying for people for over forty years!

When God is calling us to prayer, He wants us to pray in the ways that He directs. His Voice speaks through His Spirit to direct us in intercession. It is our duty to pray according to His will, not according to human wisdom.

Many people who hear from God work out plans of prayer, as though God doesn't know what to do with the needs He asks them to pray for. We must remember that we are conduits between the spiritual and physical dimensions. What is in the heavenly dimension will flow to this dimension through us. God has willed it to work that way. It is through humanity that His will is called to Earth. His will flows through me as His Presence rises from deep with my heart.

For a long time, humanity looked at God as someone who is around to take care of us. Some taught that the most important thing to God was to be sure Heaven would be populated. This, however, is only a part of the picture. God is not waiting to populate Heaven; He wants to bring Heaven to this planet. He wants to teach us to pray, so His will can be done on Earth as it is done in Heaven.

His will on Earth includes health and well-being for His children, and it includes the things He wants us to intercede for. The truth is that this includes far more than we could ever know how to pray for.

INTERCESSORS LEARN TO TRUST

An exciting by-product of intercession is the discovery of the determination of the Holy Spirit to do what He wants to do when and how He wants to do it. Intercessors soon discover that truth in a very real way, and they learn that the Holy Spirit can be trusted to be at work in the hearts of folk everywhere.

It sounds crazy to say, but I trust the work of the Holy Spirit in the folk I intercede for. I really do trust Him. I go to sleep with peace at night knowing that the Holy Spirit never sleeps and works in all situations I have prayed for, even while people sleep. I *trust* Him. I *know* He is at work. I know He is at work in my family, including my sons. He is at work in my business, my church, my neighbors, and all those I might think are the hardest ones to reach in any circumstance. The Holy Spirit is bigger. After all, He reached me, didn't He? The River of God's Presence flows to their place of need just as He did to mine. I have perfect confidence He will soften them, heal them, and turn them to the Lord, just as He did to me and has done for me every day.

Many times when we look at others, we may not really believe that they can respond to the Lord as well as we can. This is a big mistake. The heart of the matter is the Holy Spirit's ability to break through to them. Our job is not to judge, but to trust the Lord to lead. He will, you know.

When we make the prideful mistake of thinking that we're the only ones God can reach, we may feel that we're at the top of the pyramid, but it may be just the opposite. True intercessors go through a process of Brokenness; it gives them a perspective that allows them to see themselves and others as they really are—simply saved by grace, called by compassion, and used by mercy.

There is no need for us to reach God, for we are already one with Him. He is in us, and we are in Him. Life is much better and easier when we truly understand this. We are simply learners; we are learning how to flow with our Lord Jesus, with whom we are one.

WE GROW AS WE SEE OUR TRUE SELVES

Our faith grows as we see the Lord flowing out of us and growing within us. It is then that the confidence that He can reach anyone becomes a certainty and a source of abiding joy.

As I've gone through this process, I have found myself praying for and talking to those I would never have prayed for or talked to before. Sometimes I will talk about the Lord to these "unreachables," and sometimes I will simply chat with them. Whatever the case, I become aware of the flowing Christ rising up and flowing from me. I sense Him stirring up His Life within them. Very often, He reaches out to people through me even when I do not talk about Him. It is then I discover that His Presence flowing from me is a power force in itself!

It's a wonderful thing to see the awakening of another person's spirit. This is my joy as a believer and as a conduit for His mighty and eternal Presence. For so many years, He kept loving me in my awful state of sin and disarray. Realizing this, I find it so much easier to understand that He can reach anyone, no matter how deeply they are in sin. No one is beyond the reach of God's great love.

Don't get me wrong. I continue to struggle with various issues, but the point is that God still loves me! If He forgives me now and continues to abide in me despite my conflicts, He can certainly love and gather all those He is calling today. Sometimes He uses me, and there is no greater thrill than to be used by Him in reaching the lost.

God rejects no one. He does not turn His back on anyone, and neither should we.

We must get a handle on these things if we are going to understand our Union with our Creator. There is nothing greater in the heart of the created than the desire for this Union. The truth is that the created beings (you and me) contain the substance of the Creator within us, and His creative process desires to flow forth from us.

GLORY TO GOD—GLORY IS GOD

True Brokenness is always the secret to Union with the forgiving Christ, the compassionate Christ, the loving Christ, the healing

Christ, the gathering Christ, and the ever-increasing Christ among us, the Christ in us, the Christ in me, and the hope of glory to the world around me. We must always remember that glory is never about us; it is never about *me*. Glory is always about the One who is flowing out of me to the nations.

The bad news for some is that there is no way around this truth. Brokenness is the key to Union, and the truth is—that is the key to almost everything that involves a personal, functional relationship with Jesus Christ. He must increase, and I must decrease.

It is always easier to observe glory as an external reality. As long as we view glory in that way, there will be no real threat to our lifestyle. We will still be able to control almost everything that concerns us, and no one around us will be the wiser for it. But when He flows from within, everything, and I mean *everything*, changes.

As long as we see glory as something we receive, we do not have to change. We simply open up and take it in. We can go to meeting after meeting and receive, receive, receive. As a result, we do not have to change in any way. However, somewhere along the way, we will discover that we're not satisfied with merely receiving. If we are honest with ourselves, we will begin to ask why we are not fulfilled. We will discover that being spiritual groupies does not make us into what we really yearn to be. We are still searching for reality, for fulfillment. Like the Dead Sea, we are always taking in, but never giving out.

We learn that we cannot hear God like we know we should be able to. We experience revival and fire; we have fallen over at the hands of the mightiest; we have seen feathers and snowflakes fall; we have been covered with gold dust, and we have felt the mighty wind blow; we have heard angels sing and felt them brush by us; we have received the best prophecies and heard the most wonderful prophetic tunes. All of these have been awesome indeed, because they are outward experiences of our loving Lord Jesus. But none of these things fulfills the desire of our hearts. Nothing fulfills but Him within—the flowing Presence of God.

THE RIVER OF THE WATER OF LIFE

There is a River within us that needs to flow out. We are the source of the River, not just a bucket that contains part of it. The Christ within us yearns for expression. He yearns to get about His Father's business within us. This involves far more than just following another person.

You have a destiny. The Father has a dream for you alone that He cherishes within His heart. The River that is within you—the Presence—knows this, and He is determined to bring His dream for you to fruition and fulfillment. The Presence, with whom you have been joined in blessed Union, will not stop until your Father's dream is fully in operation. This is His plan for you; this is your destiny.

Your most exciting days are still ahead, no matter how old you are. When you begin to realize these truths, you will begin to experience the Life of Christ, Union with your Creator, which will flow from your innermost being. At this climactic point your life, your will and His will begin to merge. As this happens, everything, and I do mean *everything*, will change completely.

> *Then he showed me a river of the water of life, clear as crystal, coming from the throne of God and of the Lamb, in the middle of its street. On either side of the river was the tree of life, bearing twelve kinds of fruit, yielding its fruit every month; and the leaves of the tree were for the healing of the nations* (Revelation 22:1-2).

The River flows forth from you as you experience full and true Brokenness. Such Brokenness, as I said before, is and will always be the vital key to all that God can do with you and through you.

Remember, Union requires two-way cooperation. It is one thing for God to have a plan for you, but it is an entirely different thing for it to be accomplished. Your Brokenness before Him and your yieldedness to Him will determine what you will experience together with Him. Although true Union with God is done, it is impossible to enjoy this Union's awesome destiny when we choose to go our own way and ignore the Voice of the River.

As the River rises within you, you are enabled to become a true intercessor. God's Voice leads you to intercede for the healing of the nations.

THIS CANNOT BE FAKED

Union that leads to true intercession is difficult—no, it is impossible—to fake. The truly discerning believer will pick up on such phoniness immediately in the same way that a banker can spot a counterfeit bill. Such discernment, however, requires spirit-to-Spirit contact. To the discerning heart, phony ministry sticks out like a missing front tooth!

Unfortunately, there is more hunger than there is discernment in the land. It is even more unfortunate that when hunger increases, discernment decreases. When hunger overtakes people, they are controlled by that hunger. The need to satisfy the inner craving dominates, and there is nothing that can stop them.

I can remember a time in my boyhood when my twin brother and I were feeding our mom's meatloaf to baby robins that had fallen from a nest after a late-summer storm. We were trying to help them.

Their mouths were open wide and their eyes were closed. The adult robins circled the nest in the air, as we dutifully picked up these fragile creatures, only to see if they were hurt in any way. We were definitely concerned about them!

We decided that mom's meatloaf was the closest thing to worms we had in the refrigerator. Ron and I quickly put some of this "wormy meatloaf" in a napkin and then began dropping it into their mouths. They seemed to love it; they kept eating until they died!

It was all very devastating for my brother and me. Not only did the birds die, but it was mom's meatloaf that had killed them! We were not happy. Our mother was not happy either when we told her that her meatloaf had "poisoned" those baby birds! The story goes downhill from there, but I will not bore you with the details.

Many believers are like those little robins, clinging to life, not realizing the Life that is within them. They are adults, but they seem to have the discernment of those little birds. Their eyes are closed and their mouths are open. They want to be fed, but they approach spirituality like the tiny fledglings would. They feed and feed and feed, but it is without discernment and understanding.

They are willing to feed on anything that seems to satisfy their inner desire for their Lord. This is basic spiritual instinct. However, there are few who offer true spiritual nourishment. This is where discernment comes in.

This may seem to be a harsh analysis, but it is true. I hope this gets believers thinking about their own spiritual state of being. At the end of the day, true discernment is foundational to our long-term hope of true, functional Union with God. Without discernment, we will fall for anything, and we often do.

We need to learn to distinguish the false from the true. The false will not be able to stand in the Day of the Lord. That Day will disclose them for who they are. Those who are genuine will open their hearts to everyone; they are in Union with God and others, and they are recognizable—not because they *act* like Jesus, but because Jesus can be literally seen in them; His Presence is flowing through them, and the Voice sounds clearly from their mouths.

THE ATTRIBUTES OF JESUS

True discernment demands that we look for Jesus in others, especially those who are ministering. True Brokenness results in the attributes of Jesus flowing from us and them. The Voice will be recognizable because the lifestyle of Jesus will be recognizable in their lives.

Jesus loves at all times, especially when folk are unlovable.

> *Just as the Father has loved Me, I have also loved you; abide in My love* (John 15:9).

> *Greater love has no one than this, that one lay down his life for his friends* (John 15:13).

> *A new commandment I give to you, that you love one another, even as I have loved you, that you also love one another. By this all men will know that you are My disciples, if you have love for one another* (John 13:34-35).

Jesus forgives a million times, not just seven times seventy. He used that as an example to say that we should always forgive:

> *Then Peter came and said to Him, "Lord, how often shall my brother sin against me and I forgive him? Up to seven times?" Jesus said to him, "I do not say*

to you, up to seven times, but up to seventy times seven" (Matthew 18:21-22).

Jesus is merciful when no one will be merciful:

Blessed are the merciful, for they shall receive mercy (Matthew 5:7).

Woe to you, scribes and Pharisees, hypocrites! For you tithe mint and dill and cummin, and have neglected the weightier provisions of the law: justice and mercy and faithfulness; but these are the things you should have done without neglecting the others (Matthew 23:23).

Jesus gathers:

Jerusalem, Jerusalem, who kills the prophets and stones those who are sent to her! How often I wanted to gather your children together, the way a hen gathers her chicks under her wings, and you were unwilling (Matthew 23:37).

Jesus has compassion:

Seeing the people, He felt compassion for them, because they were distressed and dispirited like sheep without a shepherd. Then He said to His disciples, "The harvest is plentiful, but the workers are few. Therefore beseech the Lord of the harvest to send out workers into His harvest" (Matthew 9:36-38).

Or have you not read in the Law, that on the Sabbath the priests in the temple break the Sabbath and are innocent? But I say to you that something greater than the temple is here. But if you had known what this means, "I DESIRE COMPASSION, AND NOT A SACRIFICE," you would not have condemned the innocent. For the Son of Man is Lord of the Sabbath (Matthew 12:5-8).

Jesus does not deceive:

From that time Jesus began to show His disciples that He must go to Jerusalem, and suffer many things from the elders and chief priests and scribes, and be killed, and be raised up on the third day. Peter took Him aside and began to rebuke Him, saying, "God forbid it, Lord! This shall never happen to You." But He turned and said to Peter, "Get behind Me, Satan! You are a stumbling block to Me; for you are not setting your mind on God's interests, but man's" (Matthew 16:21-23).

Jesus gives and does not take:

When it was already quite late, His disciples came to Him and said, "This place is desolate and it is already quite late; send them away so that they may go into the surrounding countryside and villages and buy themselves something to eat." But He answered them, "You give them something to eat!" And they said to Him, "Shall we go and spend two hundred denarii on bread and give them something to eat?" And He said to them, "How many loaves do you have? Go look!" And when they found out, they said, "Five, and two fish." And He commanded them all to sit down by groups on the green grass. They sat down in groups of hundreds and of fifties. And He took the five loaves and the two fish, and looking up toward heaven, He blessed the food and broke the loaves and He kept giving them to the disciples to set before them; and He divided up the two fish among them all. They all ate and were satisfied... (Mark 6:35-42).

These are but a few of the magnificent attributes of our Lord Jesus Christ. He is powerful; He is gentle. The list could go on and on. The point is, when we yield to Him and learn to flow in Union with Him, these same powerful and personal attributes of our Lord will be ours, and we will be able to discern them in others. Words will not be enough; these traits will be obvious in those who give their hearts to Him.

As true intercessors, we will be loving, forgiving, merciful, humble, compassionate, and giving. Our hearts will be to gather people to the Lord. These are the ingredients of true intercession.

These are things that cannot be faked. They must be genuine, flowing from hearts that are yielded to the Lord and working in Union with Him. The genuine Presence of the Lord Jesus will shine through the genuine heart. It will be recognized by true discernment in the hearts of those who have given themselves to Him in complete Brokenness.

Those who are only acting like Jesus will most certainly be found out. Those who pretend to exhibit these qualities will fail. They will not be able to withstand the heat of the Day of the Lord. Those who are broken believers, however—those through whom

Jesus shines forth genuinely—will win the Day. These will be the true intercessors.

THE ROLE OF GRACE

The word of God is living and active and sharper than any two-edged sword, and piercing as far as the division of soul and spirit, of both joints and marrow, and able to judge the thoughts and intentions of the heart (Hebrews 4:12).

What are we supposed to do when we pray for someone and the Lord doesn't "show up"? Although many intercessors cover their lack of discernment with excuses, it is important to realize that the correct thing to do is to admit that we were not truly led by Him.

True intercessors are not perfect; they are human beings who are trying to do what God wants them to do. Sometimes their hearts and their compassion get ahead of a true leading from the Lord. No matter what they personally want to do, if the Lord is not in it, they should not even try to intercede. They should not lay hands on someone as though they have a word from the Lord or are being led.

We must never be presumptuous about such things. We have to learn to discern between our human emotions and the Voice of the Lord. It may not be the right time when we are trying to respond to someone's need. We should not question Him if this is the case.

True Brokenness and humility will show themselves by our willingness to admit that the Lord chose not to use us in a given situation. At that point, it is important to reassure those who seek our intercession that God loves them and cares for them, but for some reason, we do have anything for them at the moment. The reason is known only to Him in most cases. This reassurance will be far more important to them than trying to reassure them of our ministry as intercessors. We can bless them, pray for them, but we cannot give them a prophetic word that we do not have to give.

Personally, I would rather not pray for people than try to explain to them why God did not fulfill their desire. True Brokenness and true ministry put the hearts of the people who are being ministered to as the top priority. Their needs and their relationship with God always come first. Always. This is the heart of a true intercessor.

The word *grace* is vital here. Grace always flows from the Throne of God, which is within our hearts. We have nothing to protect and nothing to prove. We are simply His servants; we are to be available for Him to use at any time. If He chooses not to use us, there is nothing else for us to do. If our hearts are open and we are ready, it is only our ego that will suffer. That is, if we are still carrying around an unbroken ego.

Usually folk have more respect for those who are honest about what God is saying to them than they have for those who attempt to give excuses. I have learned that it is much safer to be yourself than to try to turn yourself into some kind of super-minister. That is a role, believe me, that you will never be able to live up to; nor would you want to.

I have learned that it is far more comfortable to be myself. When I am phony in any way, I become a rather unlikable guy.

It is far better to respond, "I am so sorry. I do not have a prophetic prayer for you now, but I will pray that God brings an answer to you according to His will." Then I will pray for God's will be to

done out loud so the person can hear me. You can't go wrong praying God's will!!

TRUE INTERCESSION CANNOT BE TURNED ON, BUT IT CAN SURELY BE TURNED OFF

Sometimes the Holy Spirit will rise, and it will result in true
intercession, but there is no guarantee even then. Remember, true
intercession is always initiated by the Holy Spirit, led by the Holy
Spirit, and concluded by the Holy Spirit. Otherwise, the activity may
just involve empty words.

True intercession takes time. One cannot just block off fifteen
minutes and decide to intercede during that time period. Often it
will take longer than that for intercession to begin to flow. Recently,
I have found that the moment I turn my spirit to the Lord, the Holy
Spirit rises. Though this may not happen all the time, I think we can
expect it to happen more often than not.

As I turn and yield myself to Him, I sense the River of God rising within, and I hear His Voice. The same thing happens when I
am writing. The more I yield myself to Him, the more the River (His
Presence) rises within.

The only way I can describe this is to say that His Presence wants
to flow from me, to gush out from me to wherever He directs my
writing. When this happens, I know He is flowing, and I am certain
that He will do the same thing through anyone who yields to Him.

It is always under my control as to whether I will continue with
intercession in a given situation. I can yield so He can begin the
intercession, or I can ignore it, and it will cease. As long as I stay
focused, I continue to be aware of His Presence, and the intercession

continues. This is such an amazing phenomenon. I love it when God uses me this way, and I always want to be sensitive to His leading.

INTERCESSORS ARE TRULY PROPHETIC

A true intercessor has a prophetic Voice. As the intercessory flow of the Presence rises within, the Lord brings the Voice with Him. More often than not, the Voice can be heard carrying a message either to or through the intercessor. However, there is a simple warning in this: If the intercessor knows what groaning in the Spirit is about, the emotion added to the Spirit can often bring a spiritual intensity that will add power to the prayer.

Paul wrote:

> *In the same way the Spirit also helps our weakness; for we do not know how to pray as we should, but the Spirit Himself intercedes for us with groanings too deep for words...* (Romans 8:26).

Groaning, as it is used here, does not refer to the expression of pain or disapproval. Rather, it is referring to the deep feelings that reside within us as we engage in true intercession—one of life's greatest joys.

INTERCESSORS ARE NOT TATTLETALES

Many folk with the true gift of intercession have forfeited their use of the gift by gossiping about what (or who) they were interceding for. They often have used the excuse that they were just getting intercessory help, but evidently the Lord saw it a different way.

Intercessors should simply keep quiet about their assignments. Their intercessory prayer times are just between them and God. Unless they learn to keep them private, they will never be effective in their calling.

There are too few intercessors who have responded to their calling in the right way. True intercessors need to mature in their ministry and respond to God in quiet honor. There is much they can do, much they can accomplish, if they can simply respond to God secretly in their prayer closets.

OUR KINGDOM OR GOD'S KINGDOM?

Most of us will not admit it, but deep inside of us the question is rather simple. Do we want to build His Kingdom or our own?

Most people who are reading this have a genuine, heartfelt love and desire to serve God, but something has happened along the way that keeps some from being centered on serving Him. Perhaps they walked too far toward the edge somewhere and discovered that it was too difficult, challenging, or just too overwhelming.

Somewhere along the way, for whatever reason, they turned away from building His Kingdom and began to build their own. Instead of taking upon themselves the easy and light burden of the Lord, they took up the troubling, difficult, and fleshy road of human-made struggles that lead to human kingdoms, not God's. Lifted up by pride and supported by people's "prophetic words," they gathered folk through personal charisma and promises that God never made—promises that people could never keep.

When believers, be they leaders or not, stray from true intercession, fleshy kingdom-building will undoubtedly result. The flow of His Presence within will keep the enemy at bay, but he will always try to find a way to slip into the soul of a believer. When His Presence is not free to rise and flow within, saturating body, soul, and spirit, we open ourselves to some seriously uninvited guests.

Merely meditating upon the Word without expecting the Lord Jesus to flood through us is a mistake. We must never forget that it is the power of the Holy Spirit that makes us who we are, giving us everything we need. His rising within causes us to realize that we can indeed do the impossible, hear the silent, say the unsayable, and unlock the secrets that will release those who are bound by pain, fear, sickness, and sorrow. Only by listening to the Spirit in the spiritual dimension can we carry His answers into time and space.

THE HOLY SPIRIT GATHERS HUMANITY TO GOD

The flow of the Holy Spirit, when balanced with the Word of God, provides a wonderful, freeing experience that is far greater than people can imagine, pray for, or study. Truly revolutionary, world-changing, Christ-centered living is God-ordered, Spirit-led Brokenness that will go where He goes and say what the Voice says, regardless of the consequences. Additionally, the doldrums of traditional Christianity have done little for the Church Jesus is building, or for the nations or the world.

It is not a rhetorical question to ask why so many believers are doing the same things day after day and hoping to see different results. It is as though some believers think that doing what they believe is better than doing what works, even if what they believe doesn't work.

There is groaning in the Spirit for everything of God to pour into this dimension. Everything God wants is wrapped up in what God did through Jesus when He sent Him to be sacrificed on the Cross 2,000 years ago. That sacrifice permanently connected our dimension with His and provided us with a portal through which the spiritual would pass to Earth and the earthly would pass into the spiritual. We, the ones who have yielded our hearts to Him, are these portals. Most believers have not taken full advantage of this great opportunity, this High-priestly calling, taught in the New Testament.

Peter said it most clearly:

> *But you are A CHOSEN RACE, A royal PRIESTHOOD, A HOLY NATION, A PEOPLE FOR God's OWN POSSESSION, so that you may proclaim the excellencies of Him who has called you out of darkness into His marvelous light; for you once were NOT A PEOPLE, but now you are THE PEOPLE OF GOD; you had NOT RECEIVED MERCY, but now you have RECEIVED MERCY* (1 Peter 2:9-10).

Certainly not everyone will take advantage of this incredible opportunity and step into this calling; but it is necessary that there are some who must fulfill this vital position in order to accomplish His plan. The Scriptures refer to "rest" when talking about a condition of total dependence on Christ. We must remember, though, that this dependence requires us to yield completely to Him.

> *After these things I looked, and behold, a door standing open in heaven, and the first voice which I had heard, like the sound of a trumpet speaking with me, said, "Come up here, and I will show you what must take place after these things"* (Revelation 4:1).

The Holy Spirit gathers humanity to God, but He arises first from the heart of every person.

All intercession is not groaning in the Spirit, although that is a very powerful aspect of intercession. But your desire to grow deeper in your experience will undoubtedly bring you to an alignment in your Union with God that you have not yet touched. This makes *now* a most exciting time of life for you.

My heart yearns to be moved by His manifest Presence, which, by the way, does not happen all the time. I am comforted as He rises within me. I am consumed beyond myself. My personal will and desires are weakened by His rising Presence. Oh, but don't get me wrong; this is not a bad thing. There is nothing I want more than to be overcome by Him. These times of His rising within give me a great opportunity to see into His heart and understand a bit more about His love and His ways.

> Take my will, and make it Thine;
> It shall be no longer mine.
> Take my heart, it is Thine own;
> It shall be Thy royal throne.
> Take my love, my Lord, I pour
> At Thy feet its treasure store.
> Take myself, and I will be
> Every, only, all for Thee.[1]

ENDNOTE

1. Frances R. Havergal, "Take My Life and Let It Be" (1874).

CHAPTER 4

REMEMBER
YOUR PLACE

Effective believers must be genuine, real before God. Jesus said:

Give, and it will be given to you. They will pour into your lap a good measure—pressed down, shaken together, and running over. For by your standard of measure it will be measured to you in return (Luke 6:38).

The Church Jesus is building is His Church. He is building it by His Spirit. True intercessors, true discernment, and true utterance are born out of hearts that are truly broken before the Lord. They know who they are without their Lord, and they have learned the hard way that they need to rest in His flowing Presence within to find true peace and fulfillment in life.

Now to Him who is able to do far more abundantly beyond all that we ask or think, according to the power that works within us, to Him be the glory in

the church and in Christ Jesus to all generations
forever and ever. Amen (Ephesians 3:20-21).

THE TAPESTRY JESUS IS CREATING

I wonder if we really see the big picture of this mighty Church that Jesus is building. Do we even know how we are so intricately woven into the tapestry He is creating according to His overall plan?

I know a little (very little) about tapestries. I live in a part of the world that has many artisans who are hard at work with very intricate crafts. The Mennonites in our area have many incredible artisans, including quilters, weavers, woodworkers, and many others. They have preserved these skills throughout the generations by example and word of mouth.

One of these priceless skills is hand-weaving tapestries. It was not until my wife, Cathy, pointed out to me the value of these works of art that I really learned to appreciate them. She has taught me to value many of the more refined things in life, including these Mennonite tapestries.

These tapestries are made by many women working together in harmony. These ladies work in unison with the designer of the piece, the one who is overseeing its creation. When one makes a mistake that involves even the smallest detail, the entire tapestry is affected so that the flow, the beauty, and the "music" of the piece are disrupted. This, of course, diminishes the value of the tapestry. That portion is redone to restore the harmony of the piece.

It is the same way with the Church that Jesus is building. We need to have more than just a local, parochial view of His Church; we also must see the Church as being connected regionally, nationally, and globally. We are a part of something that is very big indeed.

However, if we do not see ourselves as part of this global Church, it is unlikely that we will open our hearts to see the needs all around us.

Let's consider that the world is a gigantic tapestry and we are looking at it from high above the Earth. Let's say that Jesus is looking at the Earth from the same vantage point. He sees what He wants in every square mile, square foot, and square inch. He sees what He wants from every nation, province, state, county, city, town, and village; from every home and heart. Jesus is creating a magnificent tapestry (His Church).

He knows how He wants it to be. If it is to become what He desires, He needs people everywhere who will recognize and know His Voice. When they hear Him directing them, they need to obey His Voice. It is men and women just like you and me—those who will obey and work in unison with Him to create this beautiful tapestry (the Church Jesus is building).

When His Voice is obeyed by His people in every heart, home, village, town, city, county, state, province, and nation, the Church (His tapestry) will become the beautiful Church (without spot or wrinkle).

Please notice that Heaven is not the issue here. The Lord wants a Bride—His spotless Church.

> *He used a washing of water through the message to make God's people holy. He wanted to give to himself a glorious group of people called out by God—a community that does not have stain or wrinkle or any such thing. Instead, he wanted them to be holy and spotless* (Ephesians 5:26-27 PEB).

This is what Jesus is looking for His Church to be. This is the beautiful tapestry He is weaving.

CHANGING HOW WE SEE OTHER BELIEVERS

As we work in cooperation with Him, we will learn not to judge those around us. We will see other believers as co-laborers with us in God's mighty tapestry. We need them! We will never fulfill His plan without all believers—especially when we see ourselves as we really are without Jesus in our lives. Yes, that happens too. That will silence us and give as thankful hearts, indeed, for His love and salvation on our behalf!

We quickly discover our role is to judge ourselves instead of others, and to love others as we love ourselves. That is quite a challenge for some of us, but it is the way Jesus lives His Life through us. It is the way the flowing Presence, the flowing River of the Water of Life, attracts and ministers through us to those around us.

Here is a good personal test of our own lifestyle of loving others. When our degree of revelation exceeds our brokenness, many of us become haughty, impatient, judgmental. It is common to become aggressive and more outspoken than we ought to be. When we are revelation-laden in this way, we see everyone's faults, but not our own. These are sure signs that judgment has overtaken our lives, and humility has been left somewhere in the dust of our need for recognition.

But this will give cause to invite faithful friend Brokenness to come for another visit. Brokenness will come because God's merciful love demands that she come. She may need to stay for a good, long while, for this kind of pride needs to be broken completely. She starts gently, mercifully, but pride will need to be broken.

There was a tool that was used during the Middle Ages that was known as a *contriter*. Its purpose was to take large rocks and crush them into powder. It is from this word that the word *contrition* is derived. God wants our contrition and brokenness before Him.

Ask me how I know this.

WHO ARE THE ANOINTED ONES?

When people are truly genuine, they behave on the outside according to what they believe, feel, and value on the inside. Jesus was totally genuine, and He wants us to be the same.

WHO CAN SEE THROUGH US?

How many times have you attended a service when someone came bouncing to the podium and said, "Isn't the Presence of the Lord wonderful here this morning? Wasn't our time of worship fantastic?"

Then the pastor looked at the people, forcing a smile, knowing that there was no Presence and the worship was not fantastic. Oh, the band played well, as usual. They hit every note, as usual. The music, the sound, the lyrics were perfect, as usual. But there was no worship, as usual.

When I hear that kind of exclamation from the pulpit, I often find myself feeling very frustrated. I am not frustrated for myself, because I understand the question as well as why it was asked. But I grow frustrated for the folk who came in need, seeking the Lord, needing to be met by Him. A question like that is filled with a sense of guilt and unworthiness because they didn't experience the Presence.

Even if the congregation had no guilt over them, there was no sense of His tender Presence in the church that morning at all. There was no flowing of the River of God, and no angels were singing. The worship leader or pastor simply tried to stir the emotions of the congregation.

Those in charge felt impelled to make those assertions in order to bring some level of validity to the meeting. In so doing, however, they didn't understand that their need for legitimacy came at a great cost.

All too often, many in the congregation leave thinking that, if they cannot sense the Presence, they do not qualify as people who really know God. This must be a disheartening experience. Most certainly, they leave feeling disappointed, if not disillusioned altogether. So many genuine, God-seeking folk leave the meeting feeling *worse* than they did when they arrived. It is no wonder they don't want to go back! I wouldn't either! I would be so glad I was just passing through.

God said, *"Do not touch My anointed ones, and do My prophets no harm"* (1 Chron. 16:22). This is a powerful verse that refers to all believers (we are the "anointed ones"), not just to the leaders. The Blood of Jesus has paid the price for everyone, all God's children who form the priesthood of the believers; we are His anointed ones.

The Lord commands us not to touch His anointed ones and to do His prophets no harm. This means we are not to harm, take advantage of, use, abuse, steal from, deceive, lie to, or do any other hurtful action to anyone who is a believer in Jesus Christ. Whether they are leaders or followers, we are not to touch any of the blood-washed saints of God.

When fleshy tactics are employed to "build God's Kingdom," people are building their own kingdoms, not God's. They do it at the cost of the saints, the called-out ones of the Lord. Jesus does not need help from our fleshy stuff to build His glorious Kingdom. He does not need deceptive tactics or emotional antics to gather money, people, or glory. We must always remember this: He must increase; I must decrease (see John 3:30).

Let's remember, we are all God's anointed. We are all priests. In fact, let's look at two verses again:

> *But you are A CHOSEN RACE, A royal PRIESTHOOD, A HOLY NATION, A PEOPLE FOR God's OWN POSSESSION, so that you may proclaim the excellencies of Him who has called you out of darkness into His marvelous light...* (1 Peter 2:9).

> *Do not touch My anointed ones, and do My prophets no harm* (1 Chronicles 16:22).

WHAT IS MY ROLE?

When I hear from the Lord, my only responsibility is to do as He directs. My job is not to evaluate its impact upon my ministry; *obedience to Him is my ministry*, whether or not it fits into my plans. My heart's desire should be to obey Him, for that mixed with faith is what pleases Him.

Therefore, when someone comes to the microphone and says with a smile, "Isn't the Presence of the Lord wonderful here this morning?" and I don't sense it, I want to shout back, "No! It isn't wonderful here this morning! Either I'm spiritually deaf and mute, or there is absolutely nothing here!"

I wonder if that response would be out of order. I'm sure most leaders would think it would be. Therefore, I don't say anything, but I probably should, for Jesus was not out of order when He overturned the money changers in the Temple and denounced the Pharisees.

The point in all of this is quite simple: We are one with our Creator. We are hearing His Voice. We are becoming aware of our Union with Him, trusting it and the genuineness of it more and more. It is too easy to trust another who simply tells us what to believe.

BREAKING NEW GROUND

The Kingdom of God is the forward-moving sense of all that God is doing in the Earth. The Union we experience with Him will always involve the breaking of new ground for those of us who have never gone this way before. (That is almost all of us.)

God sees from the dimension of His origin, which is Spirit. It is timeless as compared to our dimension, which is bound to both time and space. As He moves forward, He will take us into areas that He knows are safe, but that we have never seen before.

Our tendency, though, will always be to go back to our safe places—what Dan Cutrona calls "defaults"—those things we have been taught in the past, those things we believe are safe. The only problem with "safe" is that it is usually not forward-moving; it is backward. Dan teaches that defaults are the reason we resist experiencing the new things God wants to show us. We always want to go back to our comfort zones.

Let me give you a brief example. Some time ago, I resisted the inner urge to call a friend whom I had tried unsuccessfully to reach. I had called his office numerous times in order to discuss an opportunity that I knew he would find exciting. I had worked hard on his behalf and, although he had not asked me to, I was so eager to tell him about it. Even so, I never received a call back. It was very perplexing and frustrating to me.

Finally, I received a call from his harried secretary. She told me that he was vacationing with his family in the western Canadian Rockies. She asked me if my friend should go for a better cell-phone signal or whether the call could wait. I was somewhat embarrassed by this and said, "Of course it can wait."

My problem was that I had been overenthusiastic about this conversation. Eventually, his secretary told me that he would call after he got back from his vacation. However, he never called!

Nonetheless, my inner urge persisted. I knew why I had to talk to him. I had to "face the music." I had to apologize for interrupting his vacation. The fact was that now I did not want to face my old friend. In spite of all this, one morning I grabbed the cell phone and called him before I got out of bed.

I was truly amazed to hear him say, "Hey, Don, the Lord's been telling me to call you for two weeks, and I've been resisting Him. I figured you've been having heart trouble again, and I was afraid to hear about it. So sorry. How are you?"

Without relating the entire conversation, let me say that I learned a simple lesson that day. Both of us were functioning from our own defaults, out of our past experiences, and, as a result, we both missed what God wanted, big time. I apologized and we both laughed about our hesitancy and reluctance. The Lord showed us what He wanted, which was a far different thing than our defaults.

I renewed my commitment to look forward, think forward, believe forward, and listen carefully before taking something from yesterday and making the assumption that God was feeding me leftovers instead of giving me something new and exciting.

In a manner of speaking, defaults are nothing more than yesterday's dinners. They may be what we needed yesterday, but they are not what will lead us into Union now. They are certainly not going to take us to the place where we can freely give ourselves to Him so that His Kingdom can be freely established through us on this planet.

It is now so much easier (I think…I hope) for me to point my finger into the unknown and say, "Wagons, ho!" I may not know exactly how to get "there," but I am certain that He is taking me there, and I am fully certain that He is there with a reality and a fullness that I have never experienced before.

I am also certain that the possibilities of changing the world in this real-time dimension depend largely on our willingness to die to ourselves in time and space in order to become one with the One who created us and with whom we are in Union.

This Union unites His dimension with our time and space, where He has determined He will establish His Kingdom through simple folk like you and me. When we give in to Him, everything in His dimension flows into our dimension, through us. His Voice, which could only be heard in Spirit, can now be heard in time and space through us. How incredible is that?

THE RISING OF THE UNION WITHIN

Talk about the genuine! As God's people, we may be entrepreneurs, educators, politicians, entertainers, moviemakers, publishers, philosophers, teachers, and so forth, but we won't do our work through the intellect or strength of people alone. We do it through Union with our Creator.

This is a Union we already have, but many may not be aware of it yet. So many people can't wait to be "raptured out," but I can't wait to see His Kingdom fully established right here on Earth. That would truly be rapturous.

> *Then the seventh angel sounded; and there were loud voices in heaven, saying, "The kingdom of the world has become the kingdom of our Lord and of His Christ; and He will reign forever and ever"* (Revelation 11:15).

The witness of the Holy Spirit within is the rising of the Union within. Remember what Jesus prayed:

> *I do not ask on behalf of these alone, but for those also who believe in Me through their word; that they may all be one; even as You, Father, are in Me and I in You, that they also may be in Us, so that the world may believe that You sent Me* (John 17:20-21).

Your Praise Is From the Father

> *Set your mind on the things above, not on the things that are on earth. For you have died and your life is hidden with Christ in God* (Colossians 3:2-3).

The human psyche hungers for the attention and praise of others. This is why so many are involved with building their own kingdoms. John the Baptist, however, said, *"He must increase, but I must decrease"* (John 3:30). For some, those words are difficult to take, for we don't like to die to ourselves.

To live a life that is hidden with Christ in God is to be free from the visibility of the accolades of humankind. It shows us that even though God uses us to accomplish important things on the Earth, the purpose of those accomplishments is to make Christ more visible to the world—to magnify Him.

Jesus is the central figure in human history, and He should be the central focus of our lives. We find our purpose only in Him. Our destiny is to show Him to the nations through our lives. He must increase; *He* must increase; He *must* increase; He must *increase.* In the process, we will decrease. We must decrease. When the world sees Him through me, I automatically am decreasing. On the other hand, when the world sees me (or I am focusing on myself), I am increasing, and He is decreasing.

Sometimes when I receive a compliment, I respond by laughing. I try not to laugh at the person who is giving me the compliment, though, because I do not want to offend that person. All I want is for Christ to shine and flow through me.

There are times, for example, when folk will come up to me and say, "Brother Don, you are so beautiful!" A nice compliment, to be sure, but I think, *Ha! I'm not beautiful. I know I am just an unattractive, old fat man!* Nonetheless, I smile at them, as I realize that they are seeing Jesus radiating from me. He is the beauty that they see.

I actually love it when this happens because it confirms to me that Jesus is increasing and I am decreasing, and this is what both He and I want to take place. It's wonderful to know that they have received something from the Lord as I have ministered, and they responded in the only way they knew how. I know they saw Jesus, and it makes me happy to realize that Jesus ministered to them.

WHO KNOWS MY NAME?

You may not be as well known as others, but that does not mean you are not as essential as others. Some have their praise on Earth, while others will have theirs before the Father. Do not gauge your value to the Lord by your popularity among people. Praise from people is fickle; it comes and goes like the morning mist.

It would not be fair to judge popular speakers and writers according to those who follow them. For the most part, humble men and women are serving the Lord in the limelight, not because that is where they want to be, but because that is where God has put them. Their message is vital to the Body of Christ. Their lives are living examples of Christlikeness, and they bear the fruit of the Spirit under intense pressure and public scrutiny while giving of themselves day after day and year after year.

Whether you are in the limelight or behind the scenes, your service must always be to the King, and your service is just as essential. Your loyalty and your obedience are to the One who keeps track of your comings and goings—the One who ultimately is your greatest (and sometimes only) fan. I can tell you from experience that there is no lasting friendship like our friendship with the Lord. There is no one who will stay with you like the Lord does.

John wrote:

> *Jesus, on His part, was not entrusting Himself to them, for He knew all men, and because He did not need anyone to testify concerning man, for He Himself knew what was in man* (John 2:24-25).

It would be a serious mistake to say that I do not trust people. The truth is that I do not expect from people what only God can provide. I do not require from people what only God can give. And finally (and this is the difficult one), I do not believe those who promise to me what only God can give.

> *A man of too many friends comes to ruin, but there is a friend who sticks closer than a brother* (Proverbs 18:24).

> [Teach] *them to observe all that I commanded you; and lo, I am with you always, even to the end of the age* (Matthew 28:20).

Jesus knows His sheep, and His sheep know His Voice. Sheep always follow the Voice of their Shepherd. They trust Him totally to lead them, guide them, protect them, and supply their every need.

Jesus is the Good Shepherd, and He loves us with an everlasting love. As His sheep, we discern His Voice from the voices of people. As Evelyn Underhill said:

> If we love God and give ourselves to Him, we must give ourselves to the whole world. Otherwise we would divide off our personal experience of God from His Greatness and Infinite Presence and turn what ought to be dedication into private enjoyment.

> One of the holy miracles of love is that once it is really started on its path, it cannot stop; it spreads and spreads in ever-widening circles till it embraces the whole world in God. We begin by loving those nearest to us, end by loving those who seem farthest. And as our love expands, so our whole personality will grow,

slowly but truly. Every fresh soul we touch in love is going to teach us something fresh about God.

One of the mystics said: God cannot lodge in a narrow heart: our hearts are as great as our love. Let us take that into our meditation and measure our prayer and service against the unmeasured generosity of God.[1]

ENDNOTE

1. Evelyn Underhill, *An Anthology of the Love of God,* quoted in *God's Treasury of Virtues* (Tulsa, OK: Honor Books, 1995), 47.

CHAPTER 5

CALLED TO FLOW

The psalmist David enjoyed times of wonderful insight and fellowship with God. I am greatly encouraged by verses such as these:

You have dealt well with Your servant, O LORD, according to Your word. Teach me good discernment and knowledge, for I believe in Your commandments. Before I was afflicted I went astray, but now I keep Your word. You are good and do good; teach me Your statutes (Psalms 119:65-68).

Of course, it is Brokenness that keeps me limping, reminding me of the Way I want to walk. She is a great help, keeping me on the path of quiet holiness. This mighty River of God's Presence is always flowing, but alas, I am not always listening. To be quite honest, my world is too noisy most of the time. His Voice is always speaking, but I am not always aware of His words, His heart, His emotions, His call to me.

The heavens are telling of the glory of God; and their expanse is declaring the work of His hands. Day to day pours forth speech, and night to night reveals knowledge. There is no speech, nor are there words;

their voice is not heard. Their line has gone out through all the earth, and their utterances to the end of the world. In them He has placed a tent for the sun... (Psalms 19:1-4).

I speak of His Voice, yet there are few who hear. For sure, many prophesy, but few hear His Voice. Many are filled with His Spirit, but few hear His Voice. Many, many read His Word, but few are there who hear His Voice. Few understand the Voice or from where it comes.

The Voice comes from deep within. It is the product of Brokenness and burning flesh as they are worked together in the fires of daily affliction. Just so you understand, it is not advisable to run from Brokenness.

The Voice is far more than something that is merely spoken as though one can drop a coin into a music box at a restaurant and play a favorite song. The Voice is not a word spoken by someone reading the soul of a person with words that are certain to comfort, regardless of whether they are words from the Lord.

The Voice is far, far more than words just as intercession is far more than words. The Voice and the one speaking are becoming one. The prophet does not prophesy, but is the prophecy—just as the intercessor does not just pray; the intercessor is the prayer. These men and women do not just function in an office; they become the office in time and space.

These are not the words of a lunatic. These are the realities of the fullness of Christ. These are the attributes of Jesus Christ Himself. When Brokenness, humility, and compassion rule over revelation—the power gifts rule over human pride—then humanity will see a display of Christ that has never before been seen. Jesus said:

Truly, truly, I say to you, he who believes in Me, the works that I do, he will do also; and greater works than these he will do; because I go to the Father (John 14:12).

The River of God's Presence is greater than anything anyone can pray for. Yet much of what believers have been taught over the years has limited the power of God's Presence in their lives. But that is completely contrary to the Bible that many so desperately cling to.

Why would God give us a book about Himself that would limit Him and what He can do among a species with an already limited capacity to grasp the magnitude of His vastness? That is the point. He wouldn't. So using the Bible to prove what God can and cannot do is absurd. The Presence that flows so powerfully through us just needs for us to be aware of His flowing might. That is why I have renewed my commitment to quiet holiness or separation at least part of the day so I can discover, sense, hear, and rest in my growing awareness of His Presence.

I am convinced that He is not moving any more than He ever has before. He is not speaking any louder. This year is no different than any other. It is *we* who are hearing clearer, sensing better, becoming more aware of the Lord, who has been flowing at the same constant flow, speaking at the same volume with the same plan as He has for thousands of years. He is waiting for us to hear Him.

Look at these verses:

Now to Him who is able to do far more abundantly beyond all that we ask or think, according to the power that works within us... (Ephesians 3:20).

Give, and it will be given to you. They will pour into your lap a good measure—pressed down, shaken together, and running over. For by your standard of measure it will be measured to you in return (Luke 6:38).

Many folk like you and me find it hard to believe that God would have such an awesome destiny for us individually. We remember our pasts, our failures. Some remember what we have been taught. It is so hard to shake all that stuff! I know!

But we need to keep turning to the Lord. The Voice is within. Whether we hear it or not, it is in there. If we are sidetracked by all the stuff from the past, we will never be able to give ourselves to discovering His mighty Presence and the Voice of the Lord within.

Who Cares About Me?

That's a good question. I have been beaten down, beaten up, beaten over, insulted, and left for emotionally dead so many times I cannot count them. I am certain I was expected to be my high school's consummate failure. I didn't even want to go to graduation.

I barely made it to university and would have killed myself with alcohol and drugs had not Jesus swept in and rescued me. But finding God's love did not put an end to the personal ridicule.

If I listened to and believed everything that has been spoken against me, I would have crawled into a hole and died. I was overweight, of mediocre intelligence, timid, backward, defensive, and so forth. But I loved God! Abusive comments were hurled at me continuously. When I became a publisher, it actually got worse! But my wife, Cathy, stood with me. We trusted God and plowed forward. She was right by my side all the way (and that made all the difference in the world).

But now I am convinced that all I went through was a part of God's plan—His pathway of Brokenness for me. It continues to this day. Hard as it may seem to believe, I often go to my unbelieving friends for comfort. God can use anyone to help dispel the darkness. Casting out demons hardly ever seems to work. (Oops! Sorry!) We need honest friends who tell us honestly that they trust us and believe in us.

Such honesty opens our hearts to receive from the Lord. It opens our minds to resist and destroy the illusions that cause us to close ourselves to the rising of the Holy Spirit within.

The truth is that you are holy enough simply because He lives within you. You are righteous because Jesus, the Righteous One, lives within you. Jesus doesn't live in you one week and leave the next. You are not His "vacation home"; you are His permanent dwelling place.

> *For the LORD has chosen Zion* [you]; *He has desired it* [you] *for His habitation. "This is My resting place forever; here I will dwell, for I have desired it. I will abundantly bless her provision; I will satisfy her needy with bread"* (Psalms 132:13-15).

When the Bible refers to Zion, it is referring to people—to you. God has chosen you, and He has desired you. He will bless you. He will satisfy your needs. He will bless you with good things. In light of this, why should we believe the bad things that people say about us when God has spoken blessings over us? Let's trust God together. Even though we will have hard times, it is not because we have done bad things. God is not punishing us. He is helping us to mature. He loves us, always, always, always.

I am saying all this because Jesus has a lot He wants to say to you and through you. His mighty Presence should be flowing through you. His Voice has much to speak through you. He does not want you to be stuck in fear, sorrow, or guilt. God wants to rise in you.

We limit what He can say to us and do through us by what we believe about ourselves. Get into the Word and begin to believe what God says about you. Get together with those who believe in you and begin to believe what they say about you. Stay away from those who don't like you, are jealous of you, envy you, or fear you. Stick with family and friends who strengthen you with their words and prayers.

No Buffering the Suffering

Suffering plays a vital part in releasing God's Presence so that He will rise within us. People, by nature, want everything for nothing. We fail to understand that everything costs something. Someone has to pay for it. It is certain that Jesus has paid a tremendous price. It is also certain that this priceless gift is given to the human heart that has to be surrendered to God in order for it to be released to express the fullness of His Life and power.

Over the years, it never occurred to me to ask why there is suffering in my life or why I had to suffer. I have always assumed that I am in the crucible of His creation. Death works in me so life can work in others. One thing I know: I am intent that Christ be formed in me. I wake up each morning with the expectation that He will be formed in me to His purpose that day.

The work of the Holy Spirit is much more active within the hearts of people than He is given credit for. I say, "Throw the seed and let it fall where it will." Some seed will most assuredly fall on the good ground, where it will grow and produce good fruit.

I am not afraid to let the Presence of the Lord rise within me. I want Him to teach me, to convict me of sin, to lead me to repentance, to heal me, to comfort me, to give me strength—so His comfort, compassion, and Voice can flow through me to heal the world, to do whatever He wants to do through me, so that the world might somehow be restored a bit through Christ in me.

In short, I want Christ to rise in me and live His amazing life through me to the fullest extent of my ability to yield to Him. The very thought of it thrills my heart (mostly after the fact). This process prepares me to be used in intercession and a multitude of other possibilities as I continue on my sojourn through life, with my King who lives within me.

It is interesting to know that when Jesus came the first time, believers were expecting a conquering King. Instead, He came as a baby wrapped in rags, and then hung on a Cross of shame. In His Second Coming, they will be looking for the same, but He will come as a conquering King, riding on a horse and carrying a sword of victory.

READY FOR ANYTHING

What kind of folk ought we to be in these days of turmoil and preparation, as we see the age drawing to a close? We should be people who are yielding to the King as He teaches and prepares us for whatever He will need us to be. If armies prepare as though they are ready to give their lives, what should *we* be ready for? Can we not at least be ready to sacrifice our reputations to say what He is saying?

We should be ready for anything. With the River of His Presence within, we can be ready for whatever is coming. But the times of preparation are now. The times of learning, the times of personal discipleship, are now. Learning to hear, pray, speak, stand, respond are now. Times of allowing Brokenness to prepare us are right now.

I never want to move out of emotion. I want to respond to difficult situations by the leading of the Lord, nothing less. I never want to pray out of fear. I do not want to pray while I am running from a big explosion across the street. I want to respond to what God is saying to me. That doesn't mean I will always get it right; but it does mean I will have a better chance than if I just respond by shouting "In Jesus' name!" when I am in fear.

The forces of our enemies are preparing now; so should we. The Voice is speaking. Who is listening? Who is responding?

WE CAN FLOW IN THE PRESENCE OF GOD

I have not made any of this up. It is not fiction. I have shared what I have experienced. I have told the truth. I know for certain that what I have is not just for a chosen few. I am certain that I am nothing without Him. If He can lavish Himself within me, I can humbly assure you that He will lavish Himself within you, as well. He loves to lavish His love upon us.

He is nothing to me if He is not everything to you! His desire is simply to live His Life gently, yet completely; powerfully, yet meekly; fully, yet peacefully; persistently, yet kindly; with love and patience as the guiding force and His Presence as the plumb line in all relationships.

I would love to see you yielding to Him. Union with God is wonderful. The sense of being used and needed by Him is incredible. I am no different than anyone else. I am nothing special. I have nothing special. He loves all of us the same. What I have, you have. What I am, you are. The Christ in me lives also in you. It is simple. The forgiveness I have, you have. We are not different. What I do, you can certainly do as well. Let's serve Him together. Let's allow the Presence, the Voice, to flow through us together.

The Flow of the Presence of the Lord

There is no doubt that the flowing Christ within will change the world within your skin, followed by the world around you. As He flows beyond you, your sphere of influence will undoubtedly expand. But it only expands by the authentic growth of His Life flowing out of you. Anything else will undoubtedly be exposed in time, for no one can duplicate Christ for very long. If He could be duplicated, He would not have had to come and sacrifice Himself as He did over 2,000 years ago in order to redeem a fallen race.

Humankind was and is totally incapable of redeeming itself. When Jesus came, He offered Himself as far more than a sacrifice for sin. He gave Himself as the One who could redeem the whole person and dwell within us in order to be the One who would conquer satan and his kingdom on this planet.

To this end, Jesus Christ looks for those whom He may occupy and through whom He will establish His rule and reign on the Earth.

I love using the phrase "the flowing Christ." I use it for one primary reason. It shows how the Holy Spirit flows from us without our help! He will simply flow from us as we go about our lives, leaning on His Life and goodness.

Most of you already experience a yearning to see folk fulfilled and happy. We want to see people being cared for. We want to see children fed, warm, safe, and secure. But it is our religious training that does not allow us to focus on these basic needs.

The argument is endless as to which is more important—natural needs or spiritual needs. I will not get into a deep philosophical or theological discussion here, but I will offer my perspective on this.

As we study the Gospels, we find it is difficult, even impossible, to envision Jesus giving a Western-style altar call or collecting money as most preachers do. What we do find is Jesus giving, giving, and giving. His giving is not accompanied by a church invitation, a tract, or even a Gospel presentation. He never asks for money.

He gives simply for love's sake. The Presence of the Father flows from Him. The people in His day knew where the blessing came from. He gave both of substance and of Spirit. Most of the time, the line between the two seemed to blur. The love of God and the giving of substance were inseparable.

Was physical healing natural or spiritual? The feeding of the 3,000, was it natural or spiritual? Jesus moved among the people and did whatever His Father showed Him to do.

> *And He who sent Me is with Me; He has not left Me alone, for I always do the things that are pleasing to Him* (John 8:29).

> *I can do nothing on My own initiative. As I hear, I judge; and My judgment is just, because I do not seek My own will, but the will of Him who sent Me* (John 5:30).

WE ARE MORE THAN WE REALIZE

Most believers do not understand who they really are in Christ. They have not fully experienced who they have become by virtue of the resurrection of Jesus from the dead. *"If anyone is in Christ, he is a new creature; the old things passed away; behold, new things have come"* (2 Cor. 5:17).

We are no longer mere mortals. We are born from another dimension. We are members of a new species that was created from the Union of humanity and Spirit. We are priests from a holy nation; we're not from around here, so to speak. We have not been sent here to get raptured out or to build kingdoms to satisfy our human egos. We are a peculiar people, and no one like us has ever lived before.

We embody the holy King of kings and Lord of lords. We are on a mission to do His bidding, to allow His Presence to flow, His Voice to be heard, and His power to accomplish His will on this planet. Anything else is moot, and any argument is irrelevant, because our vision is focused and our desire is single-minded: we shall yield to the King. We shall yield to His Presence within us. We shall give ourselves to Union with our Creator so His Presence may flow out from us and cover the Earth as the waters cover the sea: *"...for the earth will be full of the knowledge of the Lord as the waters cover the sea"* (Isa. 11:9).

COME, THOU FOUNT OF EVERY BLESSING

For years believers have sung, "Come, Thou Fount of Every Blessing," but did we realize that the Fount is within us? The Fount is already here; we don't need to ask Him to come. If people around us are to be reached in any way, it will have to be through us. If the world is to be changed, it will have to be changed through us. If the enemy is to be overcome, it will be because we are overcoming him in our lives and in the world around us with the love of God.

When you give freely, love wholly, and smile genuinely, Christ pours, flows, and gushes from the Fount of every blessing within you! Do not doubt the power of the Presence within. Do not doubt the power of His mighty Voice. The Christ within you can overcome the ego within you, the neighborhood, the city, the state, the country, and the world. It all starts with His flowing out from you and me.

Allow Him to draw you away from less important things. Oh, I understand that there are things that attach you to time and space. I understand what those things are and how important they seem to be. I know that they must be done. Cathy and I had to learn to pray on the run. We had to learn how to experience true intercession on the run.

Really! It took lots of time for us to learn this, but we did learn to listen to the Voice of the Lord while we worked and did other things. Of course, we still need times of quietness as well. I hesitate to use the term "quiet time," for those times involve far more than just reading *Our Daily Bread* and using a prayer list. Instead, we actually *pray* what we hear the Voice speaking to us.

THE MOST EXCELLENT WAY

I grew up in a household where open giving was not very common. We were a loving family, but giving was restricted to the church we attended and rare occasions when we found someone who was in serious need. I remember those times very clearly. As a result of my upbringing, when I became an adult, I tended to be the same. Even after the Lord took control of my life, that part of my life did not really change.

My wife, Cathy, though, was a different story altogether. She was and continues to be an avid giver. Her heart is wide open. She has the compassion of a hundred people. As you may imagine, that did not sit very well with me after we got married. After all, we were struggling to pay the bills, to keep food on the table.

Over time, however, our Lord broke through to me. He got beyond my hardness of heart, and now I am a lot more like Cathy. I am certain that she prayed for me during the times when I resisted her desire to give. We have certainly made up for those times when I refused to respond.

Our five sons have become givers as well, for this is what we modeled in front of them as they were growing up. We never preached giving to them. We never forced them to give nor made them feel guilty about not giving. As adults, they now love to give. It brings us joy to see their hearts of giving.

Some of my sons take in families from troubled marriages. They keep extra cars as loaners for those who need them. They even give cars away, as we always did. They buy meals for soldiers they see in restaurants and buy groceries for needy families, as Cathy still does. They sponsor several children through Compassion.

Even when we were at our lowest, most frightening financial ebb, our table always had a few extra people sitting around it. Our sons do the same in their homes. We have learned that it is not a matter of wealth; it is a matter of heart, of responding to the Christ within, who will take care of us as we respond to those in need around us. He loves to meet the needs of others as we trust Him for our needs.

We have sensed Him leading and prodding us all along the way to do things we would never do on our own. In the "olden days," we thought we always had to "give 'em the Gospel" the first time we saw them, but we have learned a more excellent way:

> *If I speak with the tongues of men and of angels, but do not have love, I have become a noisy gong or a clanging cymbal. If I have the gift of prophecy, and know all mysteries and all knowledge; and if I have all faith, so as to remove mountains, but do not have*

love, I am nothing. And if I give all my possessions to feed the poor, and if I surrender my body to be burned, but do not have love, it profits me nothing.

Love is patient, love is kind and is not jealous; love does not brag and is not arrogant, does not act unbecomingly; it does not seek its own, is not provoked, does not take into account a wrong suffered, does not rejoice in unrighteousness, but rejoices with the truth; bears all things, believes all things, hopes all things, endures all things.

Love never fails; but if there are gifts of prophecy, they will be done away; if there are tongues, they will cease; if there is knowledge, it will be done away. For we know in part and we prophesy in part; but when the perfect comes, the partial will be done away. When I was a child, I used to speak like a child, think like a child, reason like a child; when I became a man, I did away with childish things. For now we see in a mirror dimly, but then face to face; now I know in part, but then I will know fully just as I also have been fully known. But now faith, hope, love, abide these three; but the greatest of these is love (1 Corinthians 13:1-13).

I know. I know. It is much easier to pray in tongues than it is to be kind or compassionate. It is far easier to prophesy than it is to listen to people's needs and pray with them. However, we are living in a great day and are starting to recognize Him and His attributes flowing from within, if only in a small way.

Our hearts are prepared as we are taught to serve others and trained to yield to the Voice in every way. As we allow Him to pour through us, He begins to rule that part of us that we have given to

Him; thus, His will begins to be done through us more deeply. As a result, love flows automatically; it is unforced and natural. It is as simple as breathing. All we have to do is yield, yield, yield.

> *Lord Jesus Christ, we give ourselves to You. We yield to You. Have Your way in us and through us. Heal us, Lord—body, soul, and spirit. Heal our world, the folk we touch, the world around us—body, soul, and spirit. Flow freely though us. In Jesus' name, amen.*

The Fruit of the Spirit Is Not What You Thought

Many people look at the Bible as being a book of rules. This includes both Christians and Jews. The Ten Commandments have been honored as the rule of law for thousands of years, but what if we have it all wrong? What if there has been a different intention all along? This, of course, would change how we look at the Scriptures, and it would certainly change the way we live.

The important thing to realize is that the Scriptures do not give these standards so that we would strive to attain to them in our own strength. Rather, they are standards that we should recognize as being the qualities of Christ dwelling within us. As we become one with Him, we will manifest these attributes.

Instead of trying to act like Jesus, we need to remember that we are becoming one with Him. It has nothing to do with acting like or imitating Jesus. Paul explained the real process:

> *My little children, again I feel pain for you, such as a mother feels when she gives birth to her child.*

I will feel this, until Christ is fully formed in you (Galatians 4:19 PEB).

Have you ever thought about what a tree does in order to produce its fruit? Did you ever hear a fruit tree grunt in order to produce fruit? Does it decide what kind of fruit it will produce? Does it plant itself? Does it water itself? Does it prune itself? What does a fruit tree have to do in order to produce fruit? Does it go to fruit-producing school? Does it pray and fast? Does it claim fruit on its branches? Does it have to tarry at the altar?

Fruit is as natural to the tree as the fruit of the Spirit is to us. This spiritual fruit is not something we strive to produce in our lives, but it is something that we recognize as evidence that the Spirit is indeed flowing within us. The Presence of our Lord Jesus in our lives causes us, by nature, to produce those attributes that are recognizable evidences of the incredible Union between Christ and us.

An orchard-keeper is able to identify trees by their bark and leaves even when there is no fruit on them. Jesus recognized the fig tree by its leaves even though it had no fruit. The rest of us, however, may need to see the fruit in order to identify the trees.

The fruit of the Spirit is like that. We do not force the fruit to grow; it grows naturally as a result of being securely rooted in the ground and being open to the brilliance of the Son. It is soaked in the waters of the Holy Spirit, and it is fed by the nourishment of the Word, which is carried through the depths of the root system by the Holy Spirit. As we learn to rest in Him, the fruit grows strong, juicy, full, and beautiful upon our branches. It weighs heavily and feeds many.

True intercession flows from the deepest place within our hearts, where we begin to agree with God. There He flows with His will to accomplish what is on His heart. The more we understand how God has made us to be conduits for His Presence, His love, His Voice,

His power, and His will to pour out over the Earth, the more we can begin to agree with Him.

As you yield, it may be intimidating for you, but there is nothing to fear. Trust Him. Rest in Him. He will use you in ways you cannot imagine. You will discover that it is fun and rewarding to be used by the Lord in this way.

Let the flowing Christ emerge up from deep within you. He will cleanse you, use you, and flow out to those who need Him.

CHAPTER 6

TOO MANY SHINY THINGS

Learning to filter out the distractions as we endeavor to be true listeners, true intercessors, and develop our Union with God, is a lifetime task; but it isn't a depressing one. Indeed, if we find our adventure with our Lord less than exciting, then we are relying on fleshy strength to do what can only be done by the flow of the Presence within, by our daily surrender to Him.

The most rewarding discovery is that His will is probably what you want to do anyway. The desire you have on your heart was placed there by Him long, long ago. The truth is that most of the things we really want to do are things He really wants us to do. We get frustrated because there are so many things we are able to do. So it is natural that we want to do them all right now! Realistically, however, we can only do them one or two at a time! But we have a lifetime! Trust God. He always opens the doors at exactly the right times.

FINDING GOD'S PLAN

Discerning the will of God is an awesome experience. It is awesome because it is so simple. It mostly comes as an inner desire that grows and grows over time. It is something you cannot explain; but you know deep in your heart that there is something you absolutely love to do. That is probably God speaking to you. A prophetic word can confirm it, but be careful of a prophetic word that attempts to dismiss the deep desire of your heart.

THE VOICE HAS A LOT TO SAY

The more we are aware of Him, lean into Him, and trust Him, the more we are conscious of our incredible Union with Him. This naturally makes us more aware of all things spiritual. Our growing sensitivity to Him helps us to respond to Him.

We will soon even learn to respond to His gentle nod, His quiet whisper, His slightest breeze. For now, these important things probably go right past us, because our attention has been given to the shiny, fleshy things that prevent us from hearing or sensing Him; but the day will come when we will have learned true holiness, true separation from the noise—the shiny things that drown out the Voice.

Oh, the appeal of the shiny things in life! The busy things! The distractions! Even the important things! Cathy and I raised five sons, built Destiny Image, cared for a church, trained horses, wrote books, and slept every third Saturday whether we needed it or not. Believe me, I know what the shiny things are. Through the years, there were times when I could not sort out the difference between the shiny things and the spiritual things that comprised the will of God. Everything seemed to be good, but was all of it God?

We had to lay everything on the altar of sacrifice—sometimes willingly, sometimes, not so willingly. But the Lord got our attention, separated the stubble from the good so we would be truly building

His Kingdom and listening to the Voice. It was not easy. Brokenness was close to both of us then…very close.

SILENCING MY WORLD

In my youthful pride, I was sure I was more than I was, even though I was more than I had become. It is strange how pride locks us in immaturity while making us think more of ourselves than we should. I am so embarrassed when I think back on all the things I did. The only ones who stood with me were Cathy and Brokenness. Cathy stood with me because love is blind, and Brokenness stood with me because love is not.

But when I began to see my ridiculousness (that is not a word, but I made it up for this book and told the editor to let it pass), all I wanted to do was shut up. I just wanted to *shut up* and listen to my Lord. I was so humiliated with myself.

"Brokenness!" I said, partially agitated with her, "Why did you let me say all those dumb things?"

She just laughed. "You didn't think they were so dumb when you said them."

"But where was the Voice?" I responded.

She just shook her head, "The Voice was where He always is, flowing inside of you."

"But, I didn't hear a thing!"

She just looked at me, and didn't say a thing.

"Was He whispering that day?"

"Now you're getting yourself in trouble. You are blaming God because you said dumb stuff? His Voice was there…is there."

She poked her finger into my chest. "Your life is too noisy. Too, too noisy. When it's quiet on the outside, it's noisy on the inside. You're telling yourself how awesome you are, how pious, how gifted, how much better you are than everyone else. You are just too noisy."

Now things got real, real, *real* quiet.

"Who asked you, anyway?" I walked away, rubbing my chest where she had poked me with every word she said, "Sheesh!" I said.

Now I had to get right with God and get quiet. So getting right is what this book is about, although it makes Brokenness painfully, joyfully near.

But the quiet, now that was an issue. I wanted to hear the Voice. So I had to get myself into an attitude, a position where I could hear Him at all times. So I realized I needed to quiet the noise, the outward as well as the inward.

Now, in my effort to limit what will gain access to my brain, I often silence the room I'm in. Cathy says that I can't take much more into my brain anyway. She may be right about that. This, of course, gives me all the more reason to silence my world.

This may sound strange, but even Christian music can sometimes be a noisy distraction to me. You might wonder how that can be. There is nothing more important than having a clear mind *and* a clear spirit so we can sense the flow of the River of His Presence as well as the Voice. Such clarity enables Him to fellowship, comfort, lead, speak, direct me. The more stuff that is cluttering my brain, the more difficult it becomes for me to hear the Voice.

Because I know this is true, I limit my reading. I do not use an iPod. I'm not saying that we should live in caves, but we do need to limit the distractions that abound in our culture. I listen to the news, watch television, enjoy football games, go to movies, and so forth; but the times of relaxed quietness, quiet holiness, or quiet separation are becoming more important to me. I long for periods of extended quietness, for I feel the healing effects of His Presence more fully. I know the relaxing and soothing qualities it brings to me.

> *For thus the Lord GOD, the Holy One of Israel, has said, "In repentance and rest you will be saved, in quietness and trust is your strength." But you were not willing...* (Isaiah 30:15).

There is great strength to be found in quietness. The fact is, we would be foolish not to seek it and experience it.

What is our reason for seeking the silence? We are enjoying the Presence of God, the River of God that flows within.

THE RIVER OF FRESH WATER

> *Then he* [the angel] *showed me a river of the water of life, clear as crystal, coming from the throne of God and of the Lamb, in the middle of its street. On either side of the river was the tree of life, bearing twelve kinds of fruit, yielding its fruit every month; and the leaves of the tree were for the healing of the nations* (Revelation 22:1-2).

As I mentioned before, the Throne of God is within our hearts. In reality, it is us—our Union with Him. The River of God, His mighty Presence, flows from the spiritual dimension through us into time and space. Everything He is and has flows directly through us before it flows outward to others and to the nations.

The Bible mentions gold, silver, and precious stones many times, and these represent all of God's qualities, all that He is and has—everything He has lavished upon humanity. If human beings were truly aware of these precious by-products of His Presence, our little planet would change dramatically.

Think about this: These qualities are within you and they are flowing through you! Harness them, and you will change your world.

The flow of this River of Life is constant, powerful, loving, compassionate, never-ending. Some call this the Anointing, as though it is something that falls from Heaven like rain randomly falls. But I can assure you that God does nothing randomly. He is absolutely single-minded in His focus on us as individuals and humanity in general. God's wonderful Presence flows permanently, steadily, and richly through us. His is not an intermittent stream, but a mighty, never-ceasing River.

His Presence is actually God Himself. In reality, He is not a river at all. We refer to His Presence as a river because the flow is in a constant state of moving through us to the world around us. He has a mind, a will, desires, goals, plans. As He flows through us, He is certainly aware that He is doing so. He knows us; He knows that He is healing, blessing, and preparing us. He knows His plan for us, even as He is flowing.

We don't always sense His mighty flow through us, for we are not always tuned in to Him. The shiny things that distract us so easily keep us from experiencing His flow. However, God cannot stop flowing. The process of discovering the powerful Union with God we already have is the process of learning how to quiet our souls to the great, flowing River of God.

He does not "come upon us." He does not "come into the room." He does not "rain upon us," "anoint us," or "invite us into His Presence." He is in us, and we are in Him. His Presence flows within night and day, 24/7. Because we do not always sense Him, we make up doctrines to explain what we feel. But He is *always* within.

SENSING HIM

I often experience the Presence rising within me. It is a truly wonderful thing. But sometimes, I lean on my own earthy wisdom in trying to determine what that awareness means. Sad to say, I have missed many opportunities. My fleshy spirit, many times, is incapable of understanding what He is trying to say and do. I am still in the crucible of change. I realize that I will remain there until the day I die, although I have grown a lot in the ability to hear God in this area. I expect I will grow a lot more. It is true that each day is a new adventure with Jesus.

INTERRUPTIONS WILL COME; DON'T ABHOR THEM

On this very morning, as I was writing, my home was a flurry of activity. One of Cathy's friends came by with her young dog, which I usually love. Our handyman was here, as well, doing some work for us. I had planned to spend the day writing this book. As I endeavored to settle down to the task at hand, two of our precious grandchildren came by to see their grandmother.

Usually I play with them for hours. I love them so much. But this was a day for writing. Therefore, I packed up my gear and went to my office at Destiny Image. My plan was to find solitude in my corner of the building. As I began to review the Scriptures, the Presence began to rise into my consciousness in His very familiar way. It was peaceful, and it was wonderful.

Wow! I thought. *This is terrific. I am going to write all day. Who knows where I will go with this.* In past times, when God's Presence was so strong and apparent, my writing was always at its best; it flowed with the River's flow.

I was very excited, got a cup of coffee, and got ready to write. The minute my fingers touched the keyboard, though, the same grand-children I had escaped at home came bounding into my office! Then my son came in, followed by Cathy's friend and her dog! Inwardly, I was crying, "Help me, Jesus!"

I said, "Hello…hi…wow…hi…what is everyone doing here?" I tried to smile, but I must admit that my teeth were somewhat clenched. I said, "What a surprise!"

Cathy responded with her irresistible, big smile, "The kids wanted to say hi to you, again."

I said, "Hi!"

"Give Pap-pap a big hug!" Cathy urged. They ran toward me and right past me to the big bowl of chocolates and cookies I always keep for them. I said somewhat sheepishly, "I love you!" They ran by me, almost breaking the sound barrier.

In spite of all the commotion, the Holy Spirit got my attention. This was the same Holy Spirit who was rising through me so that I would write great and mighty words—the same Holy Spirit upon whom I was relying to receive great revelations, things I had never seen before or understood about the deep things of "Gawd."

In a moment of time, I realized that He had come not to help me write a book or to give me supernatural revelations, but He had risen within me so I would not lose my cool. He was tackling my arrogant, fleshy ego that cannot stand to be crossed! When I saw this (and it did not take me long), I began to laugh and repent at the same time. I repented of my arrogance, and I laughed at my stupidity, for I was writing about these very things, and I was embarrassed that I still had so much fleshiness within me.

Then I saw even more. I was still second-guessing the flow of the Holy Spirit within. I had not even given the Lord the time to show me why He was moving within me. I just assumed that I knew why, and I moved from that assumption. Whenever I assume that I know His plan, I usually screw it up! In a way, it's like my marriage of forty years: I don't ever seem to have Cathy figured out either!

SECOND-GUESSING THE HOLY SPIRIT—AGAIN!

For several weeks I had a strong sense that I should call a particular author, who is a friend of mine. I had spoken in his church many times, and he had spoken many times to the Destiny Image family here in Shippensburg, Pennsylvania. We hadn't spoken for several months. He is a bit older than I am, and I began to wonder if the sense I had in my spirit to call him was because he was going through health issues.

There were a million reasons not to call him—satisfactory, but not good reasons. Instead of calling, as I felt led to do, I began to pray for him. Hmmm…it was a good thing to do, but not right thing to do!

A couple of days later, I told Cathy that I had a sense in my spirit to call him. She said, "Well, how is he doing?"

She was surprised to hear my embarrassed answer, "I haven't called him yet."

All my excuses held no water with her, and she said, "You really need to call him."

The next morning, I was on the phone with him. He responded to my call by saying, "You have been on my heart for a couple of months." I thought, *Well, now I don't feel so bad.* However, I knew that I should have called him before this. It was confession time for both of us.

Actually, he is more than a little older than me; he is quite a bit older than me. And really, I was *afraid* that he was sick. I have a hard time handling sickness and old age when it comes to my friends. I find denial much more acceptable.

I know what you're thinking: *What? You like denial? How immature can you be?* You're right. Please pray for me.

I asked him, "So, how are you feeling? How is your heart?"

"Great!" he said. "I am feeling great. I'm traveling and preaching, doing just great. How are you, Don?"

"I'm OK," I said. "I am still alive and giving Cathy all the trouble I can!" We both laughed. Then there was an uncomfortable pause in the conversation. We broke the pause with more laughter. Both of us realized that we'd misunderstood the Holy Spirit's prompting to get in touch. We each thought it was because the other had bad news about his health.

Now don't get all religious on me and judge me about my reluctance to call this guy. When you are a million years old, you will learn what it feels like to talk about clogged arteries, brain tumors, knee replacement, arthritis, and the like. Ooh! I'm getting queasy just thinking about those things! It's not fun to grow old, that's for sure.

Here's the point I'm trying to make by telling this little story. The Lord moved upon us both, but it was not to talk about painful and brittle body parts; it was to talk about a new book project. This came out as we shared together.

I knew the Lord was leading me, but I had tried to figure Him out. I had not given Him time to speak to me. The Holy Spirit had gotten my attention, but I thought it was my job to figure out why. If I had just been patient, the Holy Spirit would have explained why. My method is not the course to take when you want to respond to the Lord. Spiritual wisdom is a gift; it is not something we accumulate over time.

> *Now God gave Solomon wisdom and very great discernment and breadth of mind, like the sand that is on the seashore* (1 Kings 4:29).

> *For the LORD gives wisdom; from His mouth come knowledge and understanding* (Proverbs 2:6).

> *...to give you insight and a wise spirit. Then you will know Him better* (Ephesians 1:17 PEB).

Those things of God are pure, true, and real. They come straight from His mighty Presence that flows from within our hearts! That is how we hear His Voice.

It is never too late to start responding to the Lord. If we want to grow, we must always give careful attentiveness to Him. Pride and time are frequent barriers to this. For me, though, the barrier comes in the form of assuming I know what God wants before I give Him time to speak to me.

CLEANSING THE BODY, SOUL, AND SPIRIT

I cannot imagine what all I have missed by not hearing God's Voice. There is nothing I can do about that. But there *is* something I can do right now. My narrow thinking and traditional viewpoints won't stop me anymore, by God's grace! True disciples need to have open hearts and open minds in order to discover the depth of their Union with God.

Union with God is a synchronous and harmonious flow of thought and activity with God. This is not religion and this is not a default. It is a give-and-take flow of emotion, ideas, actions, passion, determination, goals, and commitment. Such openness leads us into a discovery of such a depth of His Presence that it would be very hard to want to turn away.

Union is not some kind of mystical, head-in-the-clouds, useless lifestyle. It does not only occur in a monastery or a prayer closet. If that were the case, it would be of no value whatsoever. Union must work in the real world. It must function among the needy, the lost, the sick, and among all those who are seeking a fulfilling reason for living.

As Jesus demonstrated so clearly, Union flows freely through us like a mighty River to a parched desert land that needs the Waters of Life and eternal nourishment that are flowing from us. It is this River of His Presence that will forever feed the hungry, both naturally and spiritually. There is no end to the needs of people in the world around us, and there is no end to the flow of the mighty River of the Water of Life. It keeps on flowing with great and thunderous determination through you and me. Brokenness helps us to see the unending supply of who flows within us.

Believe it or not, it is never our ability to preach that will gather the masses. It is simply the flowing of the Lord Himself that will cause the masses to recognize that there is, indeed, a Life that has an eternal origin, a Life that the world, the enemy, and people cannot extinguish. This Life, flowing from the believer, is what the world will see. The nations will run to this Life, finding true peace, safety, and most of all, God's personal, unfailing love.

It will come about in the last days that the mountain of the house of the LORD will be established as the chief of the mountains. It will be raised above the hills, and the peoples will stream to it. Many nations will come and say, "Come and let us go up to the mountain of the LORD and to the house of the God of Jacob, that He may teach us about His ways and that we may walk in His paths." For from Zion will go forth the law, even the word of the LORD from Jerusalem (Micah 4:1-2).

THE PRESENCE, TRUE INTERCESSION

Humanity lives in the dimension of time and space without the sense that there is anything beyond what they can reason or understand with their five physical senses. Science, medicine, academia, and philosophy have turned away from any possibility that there is a reality that goes beyond this dimension. Anyone who believes in the after-life and the reality of God is considered small-minded. Some will even say that these folk are unfit to raise children. To them, the faith of these "misfits" is preposterous, worship (of God) is unnecessary, and life ends with death.

The concentration on reason and the five physical senses has become the major focus in schools, the media, government, and even in some churches. As a result, the realm of the spirit world has been able to run amok over most of the world. There is no discernment and no way of discovering what is actually known, occurring, and controlling the leaders over a nation, a city, a church, or even a home.

Such governing spirits do exist, however, and there is a way to discern their existence and their influence.

True discernment is the key to the freeing of a nation from the enemy's work on the Earth. True discernment, from the flowing Presence with the power of the Holy Spirit, will release God's people to serve the Lord Jesus in His Kingdom-building plans.

His Kingdom needs to flourish in the hearts of all people, but the blindness of nations has opened the heavens to demonic influences of all sorts. This can only be halted by the rising of the Presence, which carries His Voice, in believers who see and understand the work of the Holy Spirit in the land.

Folk who understand Union are broken in personal, self-centered ego. Therefore, they also understand gentleness and patience. They know that they must be faithful. They understand that their spirits, filled with the Holy Spirit, form the wall against the flood of demonic influences in the world today. As they allow the Presence to flow in their daily lives, the Lord rebukes the enemy of God's plan.

These believers respond to Him alone. They do not respond to the anger or the impatience or the fleshy needs of the people around them. Their focus is on responding to God in His timing, not their own timing (which most frequently comes from people's own sense of frustration). Neither do they respond to their own need for ministry accolades. They simply wait upon the Lord, even when other less patient folk move ahead.

> Yet those who wait for the LORD will gain new strength; they will mount up with wings like eagles, they will run and not get tired, they will walk and not become weary (Isaiah 40:31).

True discernment takes time and patience. It requires deep inner peace, dedication, patience, and above all, spiritual wisdom. True discernment seldom draws from the past. It rarely requires foundations from previous denominational studies. If you will recall, Solomon's wisdom was a gift from God. Even as a young boy, kings and queens from the known world came to seek his wisdom.

Discernment is much like that. It rises into a person's heart and provides knowledge that could not be known in any other way than through God's intervention. Those who are familiar with discernment cannot and will not be rushed by fleshy concerns. True discernment flows at its own pace and is often subject to the discerner's willingness and softness of heart.

For instance, there are times in the Spirit when I can hear a pin drop in a hurricane. There are other times when I would not hear a window break on a quiet evening. The goal, of course, is to hear from the Lord, not to perform. If I feel rushed, forced, or expected to perform, I cannot possibly intercede properly. I am only human. Intercession is for the closet, and it takes place between the Lord and me. It can also be for me and for others who are of the same spirit with me. The heart of a true intercessor is always responding to the Spirit within. Any other kind of prayer is a noisy gong or a clanging cymbal.

True intercessors have learned to discern God's will from other shiny stuff around them. True intercession yields to the Presence and then the Voice of God.

I love this prayer that was written by A.W. Tozer:

> Father, I want to know Thee, but my coward heart fears to give up its toys. I cannot part with them without inward bleeding, and I do not try to hide from Thee the terror of the parting. I come trembling, but I do come. Please root from my heart all those things which I have cherished so long and which have become a very part of my living self, so that Thou mayest enter and dwell there without a rival. Then

shalt Thou make the place of Thy feet glorious. Then shall my heart have no need of the sun to shine in it, for Thyself wilt be the light of it, and there shall be no night there. In Jesus' name, Amen.[1]

Endnote

1. A.W. Tozer, *The Pursuit of God* (Harrisburg, PA: Christian Publications, 1948); http://www.theboc.com/freestuff/ awtozer/books/the_pursuit_of_god/bless_possess_nothing.html (accessed July 26, 2012).

CHAPTER 7

QUIET ANARCHY

This is the word that many folk fear. If you are one of those people who fear this word, close this book and go home. I am sorry. You are not a world-changer.

But I hope this makes you angry. Because if it does, there is hope for you. If a word like *anarchy* makes you fearful, how will you give up your life? Your reputation? Your friends? Your denominational affiliation? The system of religion will not give in to you. It will not yield to you, or to the Voice.

> *Truly, truly, I say to you, when you were younger, you used to gird yourself and walk wherever you wished; but when you grow old, you will stretch out your hands and someone else will gird you, and bring you where you do not wish to go* (John 21:18).

The days ahead will not get easier, but more difficult. It will not be God's judgment, as many believers shamefully hope for, but it will be a sign of the close of the age. Things will get tough. They will. Some believers will wonder where God is only because they will not have found Him as their Hiding Place. But other believers will be used by God's Voice in ways I cannot even say for I cannot imagine them. These believers will be hiding places for many, many people.

The nation, the world, will need the Voice of God. The prophets must take a fresh look at themselves right now. When they utter, "Thus says the Lord," are they certain they are not saying, "Thus says the soul"? The soul will not save; the soul will not deliver. The Church Jesus is building requires an emergence of truth-speaking prophets who will not merely speak words, but *be* words to the nations. The Voice speaks words of true comfort, true power, true direction, true conviction.

HERESY, IMMATURITY, OR TRUTH?

At one time, such anarchy was seen as pure heresy, rebellion, and immaturity. At one time, though, anarchy was a way of life for all those who truly loved God and sought diligently for a greater truth; to be a believer in Jesus was to openly oppose the government in power.

Even today, in many parts of the world, to be a believer in Jesus is to be considered an anarchist, one who is in set opposition to the government. Believers are hunted even though, according to the teachings of Jesus, they cannot possibly be anarchists, except, of course, when we are speaking of the systems that keep believers away from expressing the flowing Presence within.

There are many believers who are driven by a deep, burning desire that few seem to have and even fewer understand.

At one time in Christian history, might I say, even today, it is not considered to be the duty of the average believer to examine, question, or rethink the things that are taught from the pulpits and in Sunday school classes around the world. The leaders insist that these things simply be accepted. It is generally accepted that those in authority are regarded as the ones who are educated, trained, anointed, and called to the ministry. Everyone else is usually expected to follow their teaching and the rules laid down by the organization.

BELIEVER'S PRIESTHOOD

But there is another priesthood. There is another calling to every believer, regardless of training, education, or background. The priesthood of the believer is the priesthood of our Lord who dwells within. Aaron performed the duties of the Outer Court of the ancient Temple of Israel. Levi was responsible for the work of the Holy Place in the same Temple. The Levites were also responsible for the work of the Most Holy Place until the Messiah was to come. At that point, the Messiah was to take up His role as Priest of the Most Holy Place in the Temple of ancient Israel.

This Priest, whose name is Melchizedek, is the priesthood of Christ, of which there is only one member, Christ Himself.

> *The LORD has sworn and will not change His mind, "You are a priest forever according to the order of Melchizedek." The Lord is at Your right hand; He will shatter kings in the day of His wrath* (Psalms 110:4-5).

Since we are in Him and He is in us, we too are of the same priesthood. This is the same priesthood taught by Peter:

> *But you are A CHOSEN RACE, A royal PRIESTHOOD, A HOLY NATION, A PEOPLE FOR God's OWN POSSESSION, so that you may proclaim the excellencies of Him who has called you out of darkness into His marvelous light...* (1 Peter 2:9).

This is the priesthood of the believer, and it is the priesthood recognized by the Holy Spirit. The fivefold ministries are the gift ministries given to the Church to train and release the priesthood of the believer to do the work of the believer. This priesthood is intended to minister to the world in every way God puts it on their individual hearts to do so.

They need to be trained and freed up to do so. If they are not released to minister according to God's heart within them, they will most likely flee the nest to do the will of God. They are not rebellious or hateful. They are just burning with the passion God gave them to fulfill their destinies. Melchizedek stands in the Presence and ministers there, the only priest that is called to do so. This priesthood must be about its Father's business, one way or another.

The Holy Spirit cannot be controlled, suppressed, or directed. Some would say that the anarchists are simply causing trouble for some congregations and most denominations. Upon closer examination, however, it is clear that something is happening that is not of this world; it is beyond the control of us human beings. God is churning in the hearts of humankind without asking humanity's permission, just as He did two millennia ago.

Humanity did not start this God-churned restlessness, and humanity cannot stop it. The old imprimaturs of Catholicism and Protestantism will no longer be important, and people will soon realize that they are altogether unnecessary. It is time for those who are sensing the Presence, the burning of Him within, to simply respond by saying, "Yes" to what God is churning inside of them.

Something is occurring in time and space that the old keepers of religion had not expected. They had not dreamed that this could or would happen. There is something eternal and unstoppable in the hearts of those who have not been able to reconcile what they have heard from the pulpit with what they are hearing in their hearts. The stirring of the hearts of those who are hungry for the Presence cannot be contained any longer. The passion of God-hungry believers is tearing down long-established bastions of religious dominance and control. Quiet anarchy is overthrowing the establishment.

The truth is that most shove His voice into doctrinal belief systems, so we seldom really hear *His* voice. Most call sermons His voice, but they are trying to convince the world that their ways of believing are the right ways.

God help us.

TRUE DISCERNMENT IS EMERGING

Discernment, mercy, compassion, forgiveness—qualities of our Lord that grow well together in the hearts of believers, are watered well by the River of His Presence that flows so abundantly through all who call upon the Lord. Indeed, true discernment is beautifully intertwined with the fruit that promises discernment is used in the gentlest expression of love and healing.

All other discernment is merely the reading of the soul that anyone can do with a little quietness and listening. Correctness of soulish spiritual reading alone is never a sign that one is hearing by the Spirit of God. "Spirit and truth" must always flow together. Genuine fruit of the Spirit would never allow us to deliver or use discernment in a way that would harm anyone, either believers as we define them or not; either those who "deserve it" or not; either those whom "God is rebuking" or not. *"Take My yoke upon you and learn from Me, for I am gentle and humble in heart, and YOU WILL FIND REST FOR YOUR SOULS. For My yoke is easy and My burden is light"* (Matt. 11:29-30).

If true discernment were allowed to thrive in the assembly of believers, the counterfeits among us would become quite evident. Not because they would be pointed out in public, but because they would be approached in private, as the Scripture teaches.

DISCERNMENT IS NOT JUDGMENT

To the immature, this section on discernment is a good opportunity to judge everyone they dislike. But I am not talking about revenge or about any other fleshy response to true discernment. The fruit of the Spirit are without a doubt the monitors and guide of all we do in Christ, especially when talking about our response to discernment. When discernment rises in your heart, this verse must also rise in your heart; if it does not, you need to seriously question what you have heard. Galatians 5:22-23 says: *"But **the fruit of the Spirit** is love, joy, peace, patience, kindness, goodness, faithfulness, gentleness, self-control; against such things there is no law."*

Moving by the Presence is serious business. When you deliver a word to someone, you are, in truth, saying that you are speaking on God's behalf. Do you really want to deliver a word to someone in anger, judgment, envy, or revenge and call that God's attitude? I think not. Moving in the Presence is not for the immature. It is not for the weak. It is not for the one who has not had tea with Brokenness.

WHO ARE THE ANOINTED OF THE LORD?

Who really wants to be viewed as a rebel? Who wants to be thought of as one who questions the Lord or His "anointed" leaders? We often hear these words quoted, *"Do not touch My anointed ones, and do My prophets no harm"* (1 Chron. 16:22).

However, every believer is an anointed priest of the Lord. Many people do not understand that every believer is called by God. That was Peter's point as we saw earlier. There is no difference between believers other than the offices we hold. We are all offices. We are all saints. We are all equally anointed.

To deceive, mislead, control, use, manipulate, and intimidate any believer is touching God's called ones. The warning in the Scriptures is directed to those who mistreat any believers.

As long as believers are considered to be second-class citizens in the Kingdom of God, the Church Jesus is building and the ensuing Kingdom of God will never see the light of day. But thank God, He is bigger than the plans of mere mortals. Leaders will always have their way, and the purest of all that God does will be absorbed into the bottomless pit of religion's darkest black hole. As they stifle the genuine flow of the Presence from within their flock, the reality of God's activity is lost amidst the flurry of fearful accusations and half-truths. Therefore folk are left confused, discouraged, and disillusioned.

THE CENTRAL ISSUE

This really is the central issue: The freshness of the flow of the Presence of God, the Voice, is sought out and wrestled by the machine of religion. It is clear that past revivals that showed so much promise and offered the most hope for the world have been absorbed by this system. It is as though something eventually interferes with what God is doing.

What God does needs to be carefully guarded, somehow protected so that what He is up to can continue without the sweat or fleshy egos of people. God help us in the future. May we take the time to be quiet before Him to understand what He wants so we can move forward with true spiritual knowledge, genuinely walking with Him so He can accomplish His plan.

I do not want to see another mighty flow of God's Presence go down a fleshy black hole into which all things that are fresh and vibrant are propelled, never to be seen again. As the years pass, all that remains of the greatness of His Manifesting Presence in the Earth is a memory, a notation in a history book, and a barely palatable list of reasons as to why the Presence did not linger. Usually, it is the fault of attendees, the community, or the devil. Sometimes we even blame God, saying it was just time for the visitation to end. Rarely do we examine ourselves as being the culprits for ending God's visible, tangible activity in a particular place at a particular time.

WHERE ARE YOU?

Are there some among us who will truly allow Him to live His Life through them, devoid of personal aspirations and hidden desires? These are the ones who will be used by Him and released to the nations with a magnitude that cannot be equaled by books, satellite dishes, or the Internet. These will have the Holy Spirit as their marketing agent. He knows these humble folk are saying what God wants to be said, and He provides the megaphone for His Voice in hundreds of different ways. The Voice can and will rise above every human-made method of reaching people and marketing whatever it is people have to sell.

It is no wonder that Micah the prophet said so many years ago,

> *It will come about in the last days that the mountain of the house of the LORD will be established as the chief of the mountains. It will be raised above*

the hills, and the peoples will stream to it (Micah 4:1).

The authority (mountain) of God will be the chief of the mountains (top authority). I am certain true men and women together with His Voice will accomplish this. The reality of genuine folk serving Him in Spirit and in truth will bring this about.

It will take believers who are committed to Him to even begin to reverse the centuries-old, fleshy control of the believer. At some point, there will be those who hear the song of the Lord and dance to the Voice, refusing the dance of the religious-system lords.

Courage is rising in the Church Jesus is building. This is the kind of courage and resolve that wants to be pleasing to Him alone. These people possess a determination to hear and obey the leading of the Holy Spirit in spite of those who may cry, "Foul!" The lords of this system will not go away easily, however. Actually, I don't think they'll go away at all. There will always be those who do not hear the song of the Lord and who remain content with the rote ritualism of religious patterns. Nonetheless, the Lord is singing a new song. His Voice is being heard in all the Earth. May God bless all those who have ears to hear what the Spirit is saying to the Church that Jesus is building. May His Voice be heard loud and clear through these humble and willing folk.

WE ARE RESPONSIBLE FOR WHAT WE HEAR

As Jesus arises in the Church He is building, those who hear the joyful sound will certainly find themselves in a precarious situation. They will begin to see their discernment developing and growing in maturity. As it does so, it is essential that those who are hearing the Lord will learn the foundational tenets of true discernment.

The separation of soul and spirit will be the saving element of this new way of walking. As discernment grows, wisdom, mercy, love, compassion, and patience must grow also. One cannot grow in true discernment without experiencing growth in these other crucial areas as well. Remember, His disciples are known by their fruit, not by their knowledge. But I know I recognize your spirit. I know your heart. We are one in our passion, in our desire.

CHAPTER 8

BRINK OF HERESY

History shows us that the greatest steps in spiritual renewals and advancements were made by those who were regarded by many as heretics, madmen, or worse. Even so, it was these courageous folk who, driven by their spirit of curiosity, discovery, or just plain hunger for God, opened up for believers everywhere new possibilities, new ways of thinking, new depths of revelation, and new understanding of Union with our Lord Jesus.

I'm sure many will read this book and think I am a heretic, as well. However, all those who see more, yearn for more, and believe more will need to resist this kind of condemnation and ridicule. Just remember, those who don't understand what you are doing are coming from fear of the unknown and a great dislike of change in any form. Even if you face such opposition, remember that you are not alone.

You, my "fellow heretics," are the future. No, you are the hope of the world. No, you are the necessity for the Church Jesus is building. You, my fellow frontier people, will be disdained in life; but you will be honored in death for showing courage in the face of the resistance mounted against you by narrow-minded folk.

Of course, they love the Lord; and, of course, they have a passion to evangelize, to disciple the nation. But there is an eternity of new discoveries in Christ that many just cannot see. These are things that will open the Church to new dimensions of love, power, the Voice, and spiritual understanding that we cannot even begin to imagine—and it is all right there in the pages of the Holy Scriptures.

I encourage you to open your heart and dare to pursue your dreams and your destiny. Say "Yes" to the driving force within your heart; you will discover many new and wonderful things that He is ready to reveal to you. The rushing River of God, the Voice within, will change your world as you yield to Him.

No Pride, No Fear

You who silently live on the brink of so-called heresy, arise and find your strength in the Lord. Embrace with joy, courage, and determination the path to becoming a true disciple of Jesus. Do not fear the accusations of others, but take care to be a silent listener before God; He is the One who gives you Brokenness as a faithful companion who will always walk with you. God will humble you and prepare you to carry His Voice selflessly, respectfully, gently, lovingly. He will teach you that no one will listen to arrogance, even when arrogance is speaking His words.

The reality of His Life within you will trump everything you or anyone around you will have ever imagined. This will occur as you submit to His Presence within and listen carefully to His Voice. He will lovingly teach you about yourself. He will show you your weaknesses as He reveals His greatness to you. It will be an astonishing discovery, when you see how your low points fit so perfectly into His high points. You will not have to ask for His strength when you find that He *is* your strength. You and He are becoming one, remember? We already are what we continuously ask Him for. God help us to see.

This is a simple balance. He will teach you, soften you, and show you yourself as He opens your spiritual eyes to everything around you. If you are willing, this will be the beginning of Brokenness, of seeing what you are and what you are becoming every day.

If you are not willing, Brokenness will take a much longer, more painful course.

The mirror of His Spirit will focus on you far more often than it will focus on the ills and weaknesses of others, even though you believe you can see their faults and fleshiness so clearly. You will be certain that their issues are far worse than yours, but it may be the other way around!

Do not be discouraged. His personal pursuit of your weakness is a good thing. In fact, it is a very good thing. Seeing your weaknesses helps to keep you small when you would rather be a very important person. It keeps you silent when you would rather talk on and on and on. It keeps you teachable when you would rather have all the answers. It even helps you see that the Kingdom will not pass you by.

So many would-be prophets get you all "lathered up" with prophecies that refer to your immediate calling and needs, but here is the truth: *"For the vision is yet for the appointed time; it hastens toward the goal and it will not fail. Though it tarries, wait for it; for it will certainly come, it will not delay"* (Hab. 2:3).

You need to understand—I totally believe that the true fivefold ministries are alive and well. But the Church Jesus is building needs the discernment to tell the difference between the real and the fake, the latter of which are found in abundance. So if you are the real, you should applaud this book. But if you are not sure who you are, you better find out—quick.

God's timing is perfect, and it is everything. The appointed time is in Him, not in us. I meet with folk all the time who want me to give them a word, an answer, a direction. I have fallen into that "trap" a million times and, God willing, I will not do it again. I have learned—painfully learned—that direction "from the Lord" through a person seldom works. The conviction that comes from hearing the Lord directly can give someone strength through the worst of storms. When prophetic direction through a person "goes south," though, the "prophet" will be blamed, no matter how powerfully he or she may have bellowed, "Thus saith the Lord!" It's far better to shut up and let God direct than to speak forth something that does not come from Him. The deep, inner witness of the Spirit cannot be duplicated.

Discernment, discernment, discernment! God, give Your people discernment, that they may know who is speaking into their lives and into the lives of the ones they love so dearly! Help them to not be so flippant as to whose hands they allow to be laid on their posterity!

In saying these things, I am not trying to silence the Voice of edification and encouragement that often flows so sweetly through the mouths of true prophets or those who genuinely possess the gift of prophecy. We need these words; they actually are essential to the Church Jesus is building. The more seasoned, mature prophets understand that life-directing spiritual leading must come from within the individual being led. That is, by far, the deepest touch of the Holy Spirit, and it cannot be matched by any prophet.

Those who attempt to change the Voice for the voice of a mere mortal have a long and difficult road to travel. Sooner or later, they must make the transition from trusting people to trusting God. This may lead them to the brink of so-called heresy, however.

People rarely relinquish control so easily, unless, of course, they genuinely want what God wants and what is best for others. John the Baptist was such a genuine individual. He was not preoccupied with cash-flow concerns, nor was he concerned about his reputation among people. Note his response on the day when his own disciples told him that folk were no longer following him:

They came to John and said to him, "Rabbi, the man you have endorsed, who was with you on the other side of the Jordan River, look, he is immersing people, too. Everyone is coming to him!"

> *John answered, "No one can receive anything if heaven has not given it to him. You yourselves know that I told the truth when I said, 'I am not the Messiah!' I have been sent ahead of him. The groom is the one who will get the bride. The best man is the one who stands by and listens. He is glad when he hears the groom's voice. This is **my** joy; it is now complete. Jesus must become more important; I will become less important"* (John 3:26-30 PEB).

Jesus must become more important; we must become less important. He is the VIP. He must increase; we must decrease. This is something that we cannot be reminded of too often; it rears itself way too often! If there is something that the hearts of people crave to their dying day, it is attention, praise, and adulation.

A Real Struggle

It is difficult, if not impossible, to follow the Voice and to follow people at the same time. It is also very difficult to proclaim the Voice and the words of mere mortals at the same time, for they are anathema to each other.

It is equally impossible to give way to the Voice within while you are trying to build your own empire. Financial trouble usually signals the sweat of personal kingdoms. But the Voice within is always focused on Jesus. The Voice will draw you to be a part of the Kingdom where He Himself is the King. As you can imagine, there cannot be two kings. There cannot be two masters in any kingdom. Either you will be a voice for yourself or you will allow the Voice of the Lord to speak through you.

This struggle is real; make no mistake about it. The one who is committed to true Union with His Creator has learned to live in genuine repentance. He has learned that the depth of his own personal depravity has no limits. He has accepted this as a reality of his life. He lives with the certain knowledge that Jesus teaches us to forgive seventy times seven (see Matt. 18:22), because He must forgive us that many times and more, sometimes every day, every minute! He forgives us that often because He wants us to learn the importance of living a lifestyle of repentance.

Brokenness teaches us to repent every time we sin, every time we attempt to usurp authority that belongs to God alone, every time we try to be controlling or arrogant. Arrogance tells us to run, to make an excuse, to blame others, to ignore what we see, but Brokenness will not give up on us, for such is the love of God.

Repentance as a Lifestyle

Then Peter came and said to Him, "Lord, how often shall my brother sin against me and I forgive him? Up to seven times?" Jesus said to him, "I do not say to you, up to seven times, but up to seventy times seven" (Matthew 18:21-22).

This admonition should not bring discouragement to us, for the Lord knows that we are just dust. We are but flesh and blood, elements of this dimension. We were created in a form that would enable us to carry the Light to those who are lost. The more we see our weakness and repent, the more we decrease, the more the Light of His Manifest Presence within us shines. We become more visible like a city that is set upon a hill and cannot be hidden by the flesh of mere mortals.

Yes, repentance is a lifestyle. Some have been taught that repentance is a trip to the altar on Sunday mornings, where we fall on our knees in tears, regret, and determination not to repeat that action or thought again. Now, don't get me wrong. These things are good, and they certainly have their place in our walk with God. Remember the tears of Hezekiah, Paul's conversion experience, and Peter's repentance. In fact, let's take a look at those experiences now.

Hezekiah's repentance:

> *In those days Hezekiah became mortally ill. And Isaiah the prophet the son of Amoz came to him and said to him, "Thus says the Lord, 'Set your house in order, for you shall die and not live.'" Then he turned his face to the wall and prayed to the Lord, saying, "Remember now, O Lord, I beseech You, how I have walked before You in truth and with a whole heart and have done what is good in Your sight." And Hezekiah wept bitterly. Before Isaiah had gone out of the middle court, that the word of the Lord came to him, saying, "Return and say to Hezekiah the leader of My people, 'Thus says the Lord, the God of your father David, "I have heard your prayer, I have seen your tears; behold, I will heal you..."'"* (2 Kings 20:1-5).

Paul's conversion:

> ...[Saul] *went to the high priest, and asked for letters from him to the synagogues at Damascus, so*

that if he found any belonging to the Way, both men and women, he might bring them bound to Jerusalem. As he was traveling, it happened that he was approaching Damascus, and suddenly a light from heaven flashed around him; and he fell to the ground and heard a voice saying to him, "Saul, Saul, why are you persecuting Me?" And he said, "Who are You, Lord?" And He said, "I am Jesus whom you are persecuting, but get up and enter the city, and it will be told you what you must do" (Acts 9:1-6).

Peter's repentance:

Now Peter was sitting outside in the courtyard, and a servant-girl came to him and said, "You too were with Jesus the Galilean." But he denied it before them all, saying, "I do not know what you are talking about." When he had gone out to the gateway, another servant-girl saw him and said to those who were there, "This man was with Jesus of Nazareth." And again he denied it with an oath, "I do not know the man." A little later the bystanders came up and said to Peter, "Surely you too are one of them; for even the way you talk gives you away." Then he began to curse and swear, "I do not know the man!" And immediately a rooster crowed. And Peter remembered the word which Jesus had said, "Before a rooster crows, you will deny Me three times." And he went out and wept bitterly (Matthew 26:69-75).

Dramatic experiences of repentance such as the ones just recounted can be compared to what happens in everyday situations. For example, when you realize you are about to miss your exit on a highway, you hit the brakes, make a hard turn, and take the exit. Or if you forget that dinner is in the oven until you smell it burning, you run into the kitchen to take it out. It also reminds me of when I have hurt my spouse with my words, and rushed to her with new words of hopeful penitence, asking her forgiveness with tears of sorrow and regret.

I could go on and on with examples like these. Suffice it to say that we will have to deal with this kind of repentance throughout our lives. We are human beings. As such, we will experience times of knowing that we have failed to do the right thing. When this happens, we realize we have to do something to right the wrong. We sometimes find that our tears flow as we do so.

Most of the time, however, the kind of repentance I'm referring to is not quite so dramatic, although it certainly is essential. Wouldn't it be wonderful if we were to live our lives with the joy of the Lord flowing from our hearts and the sensitivity to the Holy Spirit giving us a full understanding that we are connected, directed, and corrected by Him as necessary? Unfortunately, this is not always the case.

A family outing is full of fun and laughter. The children do not fear parental wrath as they enjoy the day, but they do know they may have to be lovingly corrected by their parents. There is a sense of security in this knowledge. Their parents will help them change and correct their course if they go in the wrong direction. The children are brought to a natural state of repentance, almost automatically, as they are taught to obey their parents.

"Son, don't torment your sister," is a common correction. "Mary, don't touch that old chewing gum on the sidewalk," "Son, put that candy bar back; it isn't yours!" These "automatic" corrections go on more often than can be counted during the course of a day, just as God convicts us to repentance during the course of a day. But we are often like those who say, "My son would *never* try to steal a candy bar! This is a Christian book. Why is that example being used?" This simple resistance is often the beginning of denial. It resists the kind of repentance that draws toward the plumb line of Christ. Remember that we are all right in our own eyes. We should never judge our Christianity by our own belief system. That is the beginning of religion, and it leads to trouble. We judge ourselves by the plumb line of the Living Word, Jesus Christ, who speaks to us about the things we want to hear about the least.

We must never fear the gentle course corrections that are given to us by the Holy Spirit. Let us not permit our fleshy pride to interfere with the work of Brokenness as we continue on our journey toward Union with our Creator.

THE FLOW FROM THE INSIDE

Believers who know there is a River within them also know that they do not have to wait for rain (the anointing) to come, because they know the River (Presence of God) is a full-flowing force within them.

These folk know that there is a Source within—the Christ Himself. That Source is not in the clouds. To them, it does not matter if the heavens are open or not. They know that God dwells within them. The River runs through them. Let the heavens be shut. Let there be a drought. Let the enemy control the atmosphere. Christ dwells within them, and that is all they need to know.

When a field is irrigated, the weather report is meaningless, because the field is watered, no matter what the weather might be. The plants will grow. The harvest will come at the proper time.

Our last trip to Sicily was a real revelation to us. We drove by many wineries, most of which did not seem to be very prosperous.

It seemed to us that they were barely functioning. However, we came across one particular winery that was green, wonderful, busy, and quite lush in its vegetation. We went into the store and I asked, "Pietro, what is it with this winery?"

He said, "Many years ago, the owner of that winery made an important decision to invest in the irrigation of his fields and plants. He asked the other wineries if they would join with him and share the costs. However, they refused because they were afraid of the expense. Therefore, he went on and did it himself."

Because of his wise decision, this winery and its vinedressers did not have to worry about whether or not it would rain. The other wine producers were slaves to the unpredictable weather.

These latter men are like today's churches that are fighting the air in their efforts to cast the enemy out from the brassy heavens. They struggle each day, and they beg God and the congregation for money to keep them going for another season. If only they knew to look within to the River that runs through them. The River is the source of the Voice that instructs, heals, restores, delivers, provides, gathers, and builds the Kingdom of God.

Dwight L. Moody wrote:

> What makes the Dead Sea dead? Because it is all the time receiving, but never giving out anything. Why is it that many Christians are cold? Because they are all the time receiving, never giving out.[1]

I realize that many will read this and agree with me, but then they will go back to singing songs of rain, praying for the anointing to fall, and engaging in spiritual warfare for an open Heaven. It's because we've been programmed to behave that way and believe that way. Even though we realize that the Throne is within, we go on living as we've always lived. Truth doesn't necessarily change our years of programming. This is such a shame.

ONE CLEAR SOUND

If the bugle produces an indistinct sound, who will prepare himself for battle? (1 Corinthians 14:8).

We should present a distinct truth so as to point the brethren in the right direction. We need clear direction. Sloppy presentations leave listeners feeling confused and unfed. While there are many positions one may take on a variety of topics, leaders must have a clear direction for the sake of those who follow them. As they grow in their own understanding, change in their position on truth is likely to come, so a good dose of humility does everyone good, especially the teacher! Even the act of changing a position does more to teach than we can imagine. We don't have to be perfect, but we do have to be humble.

If we want to remain effective in the coming days, our focus must change, and our songs and prayers must change, as well, to conform to what we believe. These changes must take place if we are going to move forward in our journey. We will need to adjust the way we conduct our meetings, worship, prayer, and talks to match what God is showing to us and what we are learning from Him. Otherwise, we will lead the flock astray. None of us want to be guilty of that!

It is difficult for believers when the message from the pulpit preaches one truth and the songs we sing declare a completely different truth. For instance, if Christ dwells within, why do we sing, "Come into the Holy of Holies" when we are the Holy of Holies? If the River flows within, why do we wait for the anointing? We send confusing messages to the folk. It tells them that the leaders do not know the truth or that they themselves are confused.

The River of the Water of Life is always giving, refreshing, cleansing, and restoring. We must learn to flow continuously with God's River, even if it leads us to the so-called brink of heresy. Growing in knowledge and in relationship responsibility will most certainly lead you to the expected and welcome scrutiny of those concerned for your welfare.

Our overarching goal in life is to become one with our Creator so He will be able to accomplish His will through us. These are truly uncharted waters for most of us. That sounds a little frightening. We must not forget, however, that He is not just with us; He is within us. That's why I keep stressing this point. The Lord Jesus Christ is in us; He is in us, and we are in Him. Though the waters may seem uncharted to us, they are not to Him.

> *Jesus said, "I am the vine; you are the branches. Who will produce much fruit? The person who stays in me and in whom I stay. You can do nothing without me!"* (John 15:5 PEB).

When we see this truth in our own lives, the Word of God becomes alive like it was in the days when we were first filled with the Holy Spirit. Those were wonderful days with a sense of freshness and a newness that we had never known before. Wouldn't it be wonderful to have that same experience again, not just once, but always?

When this happens, we will see Him as we have never seen Him before. The Word of God will not be discarded; it will become enriched to a degree of clarity that causes His Life and our purpose to be unfolded to us in glorious Union. You can't turn away from this and go back, because your life will have become transformed and your entire focus will have changed.

There is no reason to be afraid of Him, His Presence, or His Spirit. How could you be afraid of them? They give to us the power of salvation through the Blood of Jesus. They provide to us the fullness of all He accomplished when He rose from the dead. Now He is seated at the right hand of God the Father on the Mercy Seat in the Most Holy Place within our hearts. Wow!

Yes, it is truly finished! It is a *fait accompli*. What remains is the work and life of God through you and me, as we yield ever more fully to the Union of His Spirit with ours, as we continue on our journey to a city that is made without hands, the city whose builder and maker is God (see Heb. 11:10).

Too many have been deluded into thinking (and believing) that spiritual exploration such as I am outlining here leads to heresy. This is one way in which some leaders will manipulate their followers—through fear. This will keep the average believer within the bounds of accepted orthodoxy, as though it represents a complete picture of the Scriptures—a complete package, if you will. But as we have discussed, one person's or one organization's picture of the Scripture is never complete.

WHAT HAS GOD PREPARED FOR THOSE WHO LOVE HIM?

"THINGS WHICH EYE HAS NOT SEEN AND EAR HAS NOT HEARD, AND which HAVE NOT ENTERED THE HEART OF MAN, ALL THAT GOD HAS PREPARED FOR THOSE WHO LOVE HIM." For to us God revealed them through the Spirit; for the Spirit searches all things, even the depths of God (1 Corinthians 2:9-10).

It is quite ridiculous to think that all God is and has for us has already been revealed. He is so much bigger than that, so much bigger than we can ever conceive. When we explore His massive depths, we barely scratch the surface of His mighty love and provision.

My feeble words cannot even begin to describe Him and who He really is. All my attempts at talking about Him are pitiful at best. This is the God we serve—the unfathomable and infinite Most High God of the universe.

This is not to say that we should end our journey. It is only to say that we have an endless adventure of discovery ahead of us! All we find is merely the beginning of what is ahead. If we ever get bored, it is because we have, for some reason, taken a break from or ended our journey. It is time to move forward again.

Those who will not even attempt this exploration are the ones who refer to us as being on the brink of heresy.

THEORY VERSUS REALITY

True advancement in God is only accomplished by those so-called rebels who are willing to challenge what is currently accepted as the final destination. For example, many evangelical theologians teach quite adamantly that healing is not for the Church that Jesus is building. It is a theory they've come up with as a result of their studies.

The reality I know and share, however, is quite different from this. I know that healing is very much a part of the Church today. (I know because I've experienced it.) Therefore, my reality discounts their theory. Reality always carries far more weight than a theory does. Whether or not they accept the experience is not the issue, for the experience is my reality, and I will not deny it. You must never deny your experience for the sake of someone's theory.

Theories are always debunked by experience. Reality refutes even the best-written essay of the most-trusted theorists. At the end of the day, a theory is just a thesis that is waiting to be disproven. Most theorists, however, secretly believe that their theories are facts, and they do not take kindly to having their works (or their words) challenged.

On the other hand, a theory cannot be disproven by just another theory. It is only disproven by functional reality or experience. What I believe must stand the test of truly working in time and space. That is the true validation of all that we believe. It must function in the real world. The ability to use terminology that can baffle the mind, but has no place in the day-to-day reality of life, has no strength to interact with the needs of humanity. The connectivity of truth with earthly functionality in everyday life is the key to confirming that what we believe is actually truth.

The Reality of the "Other Side"

We must always focus on the Lord. This is the key to reality and truth. Falling feathers, gold dust, and visible angels are real, of course, but the folk who are looking for these manifestations are often focusing on these signs and wonders from the spiritual dimension rather than upon the Lord Himself.

"Stuff" from the spiritual dimension has its place, but spiritual folk understand that these things are only a reminder of the exciting realities on the other side—realities that far exceed feathers and gold dust, I can assure you. God is drawing us to Himself, and He is showing us the reality of the other side. Through these means, Jesus is getting our attention so we will focus on Him, not on the "stuff."

Too many people keep going in circles. When they see the feathers, they should realize that God is calling them to a deeper place of

Spirit. Then, when they seek Him, they would find Him in a depth of reality that would bring them to that point of deeper fellowship of the One who called them to Himself through His death and resurrection.

It is truly a life of endless discovery—the never-ending journey, if you will. Those who hesitate to attempt such exploration may ridicule you, but the important thing is to stay focused on the Lord. They need to know that a theory that is not followed by genuine experience will never stand the test of time. If it fails the test, it is a false theory. I don't need a Bible scholar to tell me whether or not something is true. If it doesn't work, it is not true.

It's actually too bad that Bible scholars don't subject their mountains of theology to the same tests as they use on the rest of us! But I suppose these scholars will keep on saying that healing is not for today. They prefer to rely on their research rather than their eyes! That is misplaced theology. The decision to put their studies above what they witness with their own eyes is both frightening and arrogant.

YOUR VOICE NEEDS TO BE HEARD

Some think what I've just said is a bit too harsh. Time will be the judge of that. Actually, I have no fear about making these statements or in facing those I'm writing about. They need to be challenged because they've muted true believers for too many years. They have attempted to bury the Light of His Manifest Presence for far too long.

Those who have seen the unseen and have experienced that which some educated folk have said cannot be experienced are now stepping forward in great numbers. Their voices need to be heard for their voices are truly His Voice. Their stories need to be told. I am happy to be able to report that this is happening now.

Those who have experienced the unknown in supernatural ways have a far more convincing level of truth than those who are relying only upon theories and traditions. Just because there is a PhD after someone's name does not necessarily make that person more believable than you or me in these matters. Individual experience makes all the difference in the world.

Many are searching for reality today. They yearn for wholeness and forgiveness. Those who seem to think that there is no reality more important than education will often leave these folk feeling hopeless, depressed, and frustrated.

Many theologians, philosophers, and educators are keeping people from their greatest possibilities and discoveries. They are forgetting that many people have a spiritual calling that could contribute immensely to the spiritual growth of all humanity if they were "allowed" to share their experiences with others.

TRUE HERETICS

The true heretics are those who block the reality of experience. These philosophers, theologians, and educators often brand those who are searching for more of God as heretics. Nothing could be farther from the truth. Such educated ones often deny the realities of personal experience, and they will even go so far as to forbid all possibilities of greater interaction between God and people.

Why? It's because they don't see it in what they've studied; therefore, it has become impossibility to them. They brand the humble, the broken, the hungry, the soft-hearted believers as the rebellious heretics. But they are the ones who reject the experience that Jesus rejoiced to see working in the hearts of humanity when He told the disciples what would happen when He went away: *"Truly, truly, I say to you, he who believes in Me, the works that I do, he will do also; and greater works than these he will do; because I go to the Father"* (John 14:12).

He rejoiced further when He saw revelation working in Peter. *"And Jesus said to him, 'Blessed are you, Simon Barjona, because flesh and blood did not reveal this to you, but My Father who is in heaven'"* (Matt. 16:17).

It is the responsibility of believers to hear and respond to the work of the River of God's Presence that flows within them. That will most certainly reveal the Christ in new and exciting ways to all of us. The responsibility of that revelation comes with it, though, as all mature believers must surely understand and accept.

LET JESUS BE SEEN IN YOU

Our lives should be all about Jesus Christ living His Life through us in total Union with Him. This is what enables others to see Jesus in us. This does not mean we try to act like Him. It means we simply rest in Him, so we become one with Him.

Everything He did when He walked the Earth will be done through us. This is not for our own recognition, but for His. It's not for us to receive fame, but it is to make Him known. His glory, not our own, is what it's all about. I *must* decrease, and He *must* increase.

In all that I am saying, I want to be an explorer. I want to know Jesus in the fellowship of His sufferings and in the power of His resurrection. The suffering keeps me humble so that I will never abuse the power of His resurrection (see Phil. 3:10).

The Word and the Spirit must agree, but by whose definition? Yours? Mine? The teachers of the past? As sojourners in this life, our revelation should increase as we go on, and go deeper. Our knowledge of the Truth will increase, as we continue going toward Him.

Usually heresy is determined by what we do or do not believe. Those who don't pray in tongues, for instance, think I am a heretic because I do pray in tongues. It may seem heretical, but I don't believe in the Rapture as it is taught by most evangelicals. Similarly, I do not accept the King James Version of the Bible as being the only acceptable translation. This list could go on and on with regard to such matters.

The point to remember is that heresy is relative to what one does or does not believe. The fear of being branded a heretic often keeps believers from further exploration or even studying the Scriptures to see if certain things are so or not. Theologians have used this ploy for centuries. Their apparent goal was and still is to keep believers from studying the Bible on their own, lest they discover truth that will bring people into a new and genuine experience with God. Such leaders would feel threatened if this were to take place.

I don't want to live in limited understanding when I know that the possibilities in Him are vast and ever-changing. I know that doctrine is not the only reality. Doctrine proven by experience is the true reality. If a spiritual theory cannot be proven by real experience, then it is not worth the breath that is involved with talking about it.

When people began to experience the baptism in the Holy Spirit in droves during the 1960s and 1970s, many thought it was a terrible heresy. When multitudes of people began to be healed under the ministry of evangelists, people thought it was heresy. These things split churches and denominations, but they restored vital truth to the Church Jesus is building.

Living on the brink of so-called heresy is exciting, because it requires us to draw closer to God, and this is the goal of all of life. So, be sure to let the River of the Water of Life rise up and flow out from you. It is this that will bring change to the world, beginning with yours.

ENDNOTE

1. Dwight L. Moody, *D.L. Moody Yearbook,* selected by Emma Moody Fitt (New York: Fleming H. Revell, 1900), quoted in *God's Treasury of Virtues* (Tulsa, OK: Honor Books, 1995), 234.

CHAPTER 9

THE RIVER OF
THE WATER OF LIFE

Listen. There is a New Song. It is a song everyone can hear. It is sung throughout the universe. It covers the earth in mesmerizing harmony. It makes all things flow the way they should—the way they are intended to flow—with purpose, beauty, divine peace, order, majesty, and glory. Listen! The Song our Lord is singing is holding all things together.

It is being sung in the Spirit. It is the song the angels sang when Jesus was born, when the angels let themselves be seen and heard in the skies over Bethlehem. But it was heard long before that night. It was heard by the prophets of old throughout the Old Covenant. It was heard the day God breathed into Adam the breath of life and he became a living soul. But it did not even begin there. For the darkness heard it when that New Song was spoken by God Almighty and He separated darkness from the light.

But there was yet something more divine than that! It did not begin there either! This New Song is a song of redemption, hope, wholeness, love, and passion. It is a song that our Father has been singing in His dimension of timelessness for eternity. For those who discern, they know that He has been singing this New Song since before time ever began. The Father is singing it in eternity where there is no time. It can be heard here where we are locked in time. It is sung where He has been looking forward from the day of the Cross.

The Song came to the earth and became flesh and blood. The enemy became crazy with fear. The Song instantly began to change the world. So they nailed the Song to a cross of shame, but it was too late, it was already released into His destiny among humanity. The depths of hell could not hold or destroy the melodies of Life the Song was singing, and soon captivity was singing the Song. Within three days, the Song led them to eternal freedom, and with the mighty Song of deliverance, He pronounced the once-and-for-all death sentence on the enemies of God.

The Song spilled over the Earth like the sunrise shoots its rays over the darkness, chasing it away.

The ancient prophets heard it coming into time and space, and announced its arrival. King David heard this New Song and wrote psalm after psalm, all New Songs about the coming Messiah, speaking with prophetic love, power, and clarity about the gathering and healing power of the One whose Voice would once and for all fill the earth.

No Voice but Ours

This New Song is the Song that flows out of you as the River of His Presence flows through you. It is a song that sings and sings. Sometimes it is like a fire, sometimes like a river, sometimes like a deep inner longing, often like uncontrollable joy. It sometimes feels like a nudge when you feel led to do something, sometimes as a force to pray in an unlikely moment or to speak when you should be quiet. The Voice shows Himself in more ways than can be told in one book, so we must be open to Him all the time. The New Song is the Voice looking for expression in the Earth.

But I am afraid that we do not understand that it has no voice but ours. The New Song is the Voice looking for expression in you. He has no outlet but willing souls who are brave enough to trust the Creator, Father, Redeemer, and Resurrector more than they can trust themselves. These are the majestic ones in the earth, in whom is the delight of the Lord (see Ps. 16:3). These will yield to Him at all costs. They will not just see the Kingdom come. They will usher the Kingdom into time and space by way of their own honor and subjection to their King.

It is our yieldedness that is the key to our fulfillment in this life and to His awesome Kingdom in the Earth. You and I are vital to His purpose.

The New Song is filling the Earth today. It is the song of the King of kings. It is being sung all the time. It is the Song of the Voice—the Song of the realm of all-God. As the River of God flows through you, you do not just hear it; you sing it as well. There is no doubt that you actually become the Song of the River, His mighty Presence. It is the Song of love, acceptance, well-being, wholeness, and compassion. It is the Song of gathering, healing—the Song that takes away all pain and sorrow.

Imagine this amazing paradox. This New Song is one that you do not necessarily sing. It is a song that you live. In fact, the Voice is just as well lived and spoken as it is sung, for few folk can hear the Voice, but nearly everyone can see it. When it is lived in the joy of the Lord, it is the Song, lived! The Song is visible through the lives of all who sing it. The New Song radiates from the life of a believer like light radiates from the sun. It is like the light radiated from Moses after he received the Ten Commandments, or like Jesus on the Mount of Transfiguration. *"Sing to Him a new song; play skillfully with a shout of joy"* (Ps. 33:3).

THE NEW SONG OF GOD'S MYSTERIES

The New Song sings the mysteries of the New Covenant. It is the Song that is sung by myriads of angels, the great cloud of witnesses, and all those who hear the joyful sound. It is so new, so revelatory, that it is written as it is sung. There is so much to sing about that this Song is never repeated. When you listen, it is always new, always revealing, and always joyful. It rises up through the River of His Presence and spills into time and space and splashes over everyone, whether or not they are aware of its powerful, eternal benefits.

Would that everyone could see the multifaceted wonders of the New Song—its sounds, its words, its melody, its hope, its life, and its love! The message of this Song is certainly God's intention for His people—delivered through the likes of you and me. His intention will always come to pass.

Before the Earth was formed, God had redemption on His mind. He knew His plan, and He knew the destiny of His only Son. This redemption would change the universe, and it would free people from their captivity to this dimension, offering them the possibilities of a redemption we have yet to understand and certainly experience in its fullness. All the wonders of this salvation are yet to be released and to flow into our human experience. It is a liberation that will change the "sons of men" into the "sons of God." Humankind will no longer be confined to the five physical senses, no longer be left to the life-and-death struggle that was the destiny of earthbound human beings before this glorious redemption came to be.

God released them, redeemed them, filled them with His Spirit, instructed them, and allowed them to understand and explore His deeper truths, which are intended to be more than mere doctrines, but experiences—a way of daily life. These are the things that angels long to look into, but are now reserved for His children.

Peter said to Jesus, *"You are the Christ, the Son of the living God"* (Matt. 16:16). Jesus rejoiced at this statement, for it signaled that mere mortals could be redeemed. Humankind could see things that flesh and blood did not reveal to them. Humankind was now just "a little lower than the angels" (see Heb. 2:7), but was about to be crowned with glory and honor. People could see and proclaim the New Song. The dimension of time and space was about to be flooded with truth and experience, with the love and power of another world. The world of the Spirit had been entrusted to people by their living, loving God.

OTHERS SAW WHAT WE WOULD LIVE

David wondered about humankind. He wondered about the Union with God that he saw in the Spirit. He was overwhelmed by the nearness of God to humanity when he said, *"Such knowledge is too wonderful for me; it is too high, I cannot attain to it"* (Ps. 139:6).

This New Song filled the hearts and imaginations of the Old Testament prophets. This New Song is a song that could not be sung by one person, one choir, or one nation. It is a universal song that needs to be sung by all nature, all universes, all dimensions.

> *Praise the LORD! Sing to the LORD a new song, and*
> *His praise in the congregation of the godly ones*
> (Psalms 149:1).

Sing to the LORD a new song; sing to the LORD, all the earth (Psalms 96:1).

Sing to the LORD a new song, sing His praise from the end of the earth! You who go down to the sea, and all that is in it. You islands, and those who dwell on them. Let the wilderness and its cities lift up their voices, the settlements where Kedar inhabits. Let the inhabitants of Sela sing aloud, let them shout for joy from the tops of the mountains. Let them give glory to the LORD and declare His praise in the coastlands (Isaiah 42:10-12).

For the creation was subjected to futility, not willingly, but because of Him who subjected it, in hope that the creation itself also will be set free from its slavery to corruption into the freedom of the glory of the children of God. For we know that the whole creation groans and suffers the pains of childbirth together until now. And not only this, but also we ourselves, having the first fruits of the Spirit, even we ourselves groan within ourselves, waiting eagerly for our adoption as sons, the redemption of our body (Romans 8:20-23).

BLESSING AND WARNING

God is speaking to us across this land. He is saying new things. He is opening the same Scriptures to new understanding. With this new understanding comes grave responsibility, however. That is what I mean when I say that with new revelation comes Brokenness and softness of heart. Arrogance always resists and dismisses new understanding. Pride causes new revelation to lose its power and impact.

> *When pride comes, then comes dishonor, but with the humble is wisdom* (Proverbs 11:2).

> *Only by pride cometh contention: but with the well advised is wisdom* (Proverbs 13:10 KJV).

Many search for revelation for the good of the Kingdom of God while others want revelation for their own advancement. Make no mistake about this; God knows the difference between these two approaches. If God chooses to give you true revelation, He will also send Brokenness along to be sure you use that revelation for the sake of the Kingdom of God, even though you may have meant it for your own purposes.

There is both encouragement and warning in what I am saying. I want you to soar where the Lord takes you, but I also want you to do so with humility. Once you begin to see the wonders of true redemption, you will need true humility and Brokenness.

THE CRYSTAL RIVER

> *Then he* [the angel] *showed me a river of the water of life, clear as crystal, coming from the throne of God and of the Lamb, in the middle of its street. On either side of the river was the tree of life, bearing twelve kinds of fruit, yielding its fruit every month; and the leaves of the tree were for the healing of the nations. There will no longer be any curse; and the*

throne of God and of the Lamb will be in it, and His bond-servants will serve Him; they will see His face, and His name will be on their foreheads. And there will no longer be any night; and they will not have need of the light of a lamp nor the light of the sun, because the Lord God will illumine them; and they will reign forever and ever (Revelation 22:1-5).

This is the most powerful prophetic description of the Church Jesus is building that I can find in the New Testament. Here the flow of God is freely pouring from the hearts of those who are open to Him and all He wants to do on the Earth. The River is rushing forth from the Throne of God, the very heart of humanity. This is truly the daily lifestyle of the believer. It is the believers at rest from their own labors and allowing the Lord to live His Life through them. This is the Melchizedek of God at work. This is the priesthood that will, in these days, turn the kingdoms of this world into the Kingdom of our Lord and of His Christ.

Then the seventh angel sounded; and there were loud voices in heaven, saying, "The kingdom of the world has become the kingdom of our Lord and of His Christ; and He will reign forever and ever" (Revelation 11:15).

He who believes in Me, as the Scripture said, "From his innermost being will flow rivers of living water" (John 7:38).

The hands of people are the leaves of the Tree of Life. Stretched forth to dying humanity, the Tree always bears fruit since the River is always flowing. Paul wrote: *"Preach the word; be ready in season and out of season; reprove, rebuke, exhort, with great patience and instruction"* (2 Tim. 4:2).

It is always the right season for the God-flowing believer. The leaves (hands) of the Tree are for the healing of the nations. The God-flowing believers remove the curse as they themselves stop cursing the peoples of the Earth with religion's tirades of self-centeredness, self-righteousness, and condemnation. Their very presence is like Jesus who came upon the demoniac in the country of the Gadarenes. Demons cannot stand the Presence of the Lord. Even when there is not such a violent encounter, love rules the day and people are freed from the curses that were set in place by hate.

> *When He came to the other side into the country of the Gadarenes, two men who were demon-possessed met Him as they were coming out of the tombs. They were so extremely violent that no one could pass by that way. And they cried out, saying, "What business do we have with each other, Son of God? Have You come here to torment us before the time?" Now there was a herd of many swine feeding at a distance from them. The demons began to entreat Him, saying, "If You are going to cast us out, send us into the herd of swine." And He said to them, "Go!" And they came out and went into the swine, and the whole herd rushed down the steep bank into the sea and perished in the waters* (Matthew 8:28-32).

The River of His Life carries everything that is His from the dimension of His origin (eternity) to the dimension of time and space (us). Therefore, the River of Life (His Presence), flowing from deep within us, carries all that we call the fruit and gifts of the Spirit. These are aspects of His Life and His personality. He is far more than these. The greatness of our God is far more than we can possibly imagine. The flow of His Presence within is *Him*, the Lord Himself. Anything someone needs we have within because we have Him.

> *The fruit of the Spirit is love, joy, peace, patience, kindness, goodness, faithfulness, gentleness, self-control; against such things there is no law* (Galatians 5:22-23).

First Corinthians 12 lists some of what we have come to call the gifts of the Spirit. But God is not limited to what is listed there. We serve a multifaceted God! Who He is in personality and power become normalized in each of us as we mature. His characteristics actually become woven into who we are, as we become one with our Creator. Otherwise, they are mostly restricted to a gathering of the believers.

As long as we live in the gift realm or Pentecostal realm or Charismatic realm, we will specialize in one gift or a few fruit, but if we truly understand that the River of His Presence flows from within us, then we understand that all of Christ is within. Therefore, I can do all things through Him who strengthens me (see Phil. 4:13). I am not limited by anything, for all of the living Christ is within me.

The River of Life, the Voice, flows from us naturally as we speak, laugh, love, hug, give, and gather. God flows from us as we breathe. Most of the time, we are not aware of this, because we are one with Him. This is the ongoing process of falling in love, of yielding to and becoming one with our Lord.

We have become what we have tried to do for so long in the flesh. Now that we have become one with the River of the Water of Life, there is no more need to try. There is only being. Loving has become natural and easy. Forgiveness has become a normal part of the believer's life. Gathering is what the believer does, and it happens with no hesitation, as Jesus did and still does. Encouraging and building one another up in the faith becomes as automatic as breathing.

LOVE TAKES THE HIGH GROUND

Love will take the high ground, no matter who is involved. This may sound like a hippie from the Sixties speaking, but you must remember that the Jesus People who came from the flower-child movement are the ones who began to hear something that changed the course of nations. Their influence continues to this day, and we are beginning to experience a resurgence of the Jesus Movement's music, clothing, rebellion, and passion. The cry of the Sixties is being heard again. Is it the Voice? Only time will tell. One thing is certain: The nation and the world are ripe once again for a political and spiritual shaking.

Yes, a Voice is rising among believers. I am not so cynical as to claim that the voice that is rising among worldly revolutionaries is demonic, however. The Scriptures are far too clear in showing that people are too quick to judge; Jesus and His followers were called "demon possessed." We must be very careful in this regard.

John came neither eating normal food nor drinking water. And they say, "He has a demon inside him" (Matthew 11:18 PEB).

The Jews answered and said to Him, "Do we not say rightly that You are a Samaritan and have a demon?" Jesus answered, "I do not have a demon; but I honor My Father, and you dishonor Me" (John 8:48-49).

Many of them were saying, "He has a demon and is insane. Why do you listen to Him?" Others were saying, "These are not the sayings of one demon-possessed. A demon cannot open the eyes of the blind, can he?" (John 10:20-21).

Our role is to stay focused, to love, and to stay yielded to the One with whom we are one. Our goal is to continually allow Him to arise within us. We are no longer on our own. We are not simply wandering through life begging Him to answer our meager prayers. I have a purpose and so do you. His dream for you is alive and active, and it is moving forward within you with vigor and godly anticipation.

He Has a Mind of His Own

The River of God is flowing with power. Strange as it may seem, He has a mind of His own. He does not need our counsel, our wisdom, or our reminders. There are folk who more clearly understand that this River, *He Himself*, has a mind of His own.

There are folk who will simply yield to Him and say, "Not my will, Lord, but Your will be done." This time there are folk who will say from their hearts, with repentance, "I must decrease, and You, my dear Lord Jesus, must surely increase, even if it is not in me or through me or in my church or organization. You *must* increase, and I must decrease!"

Many years ago, I was invited to preach in a church where there was a great anticipation of revival. All the prayers were right, and the words were right. The songs were right, also, but I could not shake the feeling that something was wrong there.

A young man got up to announce an early-morning prayer meeting. He was quite excited. At the end of his announcement, he noted that with all the prayer and fasting that was taking place there, he was certain that revival would break out in their church before it would break out in the church across town. The folk broke out with cheers and applause.

This caused me to know that there was an intense competition between those two churches as to which would enter revival first. Well, my talk that morning, as you can well imagine, gently confronted this spirit of competition. For some reason, I was never invited back there to speak.

We must decrease. The competition we're engaged in is not to see how we can be used first, seen first, or blessed first. I am not striving to be the first or best at prophesying, healing the sick, preaching, or writing. These things are not in the front of my mind. Brokenness is my continuous reminder to allow God to take me or leave me wherever He needs me.

REPENTANCE CHANGES ACTIONS

The things we are describing cannot be faked. God will be visible outwardly to the degree that we have submitted to Him inwardly. Our Lord Jesus will not be seen outwardly if we have not changed inwardly. It is simply impossible to sing the New Song if there is no real repentance within the heart. *"It is not what enters into the mouth that defiles the man, but what proceeds out of the mouth, this defiles the man"* (Matt. 15:11).

You will know what is really within people by what they say. The fruit of the Spirit are fused into the hearts of people as they experience Union with Christ. If that growth does not take place, their words and actions will simply betray them.

Spiritual people will understand that they condemn themselves by the words that flow out of their mouths. The words that judge, condemn, and accuse are the words that flow from the heart and defile people. Those who carry the Brokenness of the Lord are driven to silence and prayer, for they know from experience the end of those who engage in harsh judgments without true repentance.

> So also the tongue is a small part of the body, and yet it boasts of great things. See how great a forest is set aflame by such a small fire! And the tongue is a fire, the very world of iniquity; the tongue is set among our members as that which defiles the entire body, and sets on fire the course of our life, and is set on fire by hell (James 3:5-6).

The actions of people should change when Jesus Christ lives within them. The fruit of the Spirit, the true character of Jesus, hang from people like apples from a tree in a well-kept orchard in early autumn. The flow of the River of His Presence is too obvious. He simply cannot be faked. Union changes everything about us.

The Scripture says that the Presence shining from Moses was so obvious that he tried to hide it after getting the Ten Commandments from Mount Sinai by putting a bag over his head! (See Exodus 34:33-35.)

THE RIVER OF HIS PRESENCE DRIVES US FORWARD INTO HIM

There is only one direction for the Church that Jesus is building, and that is forward. Too many of us are content, satisfied to stay where we are, no matter where that may be. The Word tells us we

are on a journey, a quest; we are searching for something meaning-
ful in life.

That sense of longing will only be satisfied when we yield to the
One flowing within us. He satisfies the yearning of the heart for He
has given us that yearning. Peace comes when we simply relax in
Him, saying a simple "Yes" to Him. *"Delight yourself in the Lord;
and He will give you the desires of your heart"* (Ps. 37:4).

CHAPTER 10

THE CHURCH
JESUS IS BUILDING

The Church Jesus is building is one of progressive revelation, not regressive stagnation. It is the Fellowship of the Promised Land. Is it perfect? Absolutely not! But this fellowship is more acutely aware of its faults. Its people live in an attitude of Brokenness. The mercy of God pours from them naturally because they are acutely aware of how desperately they need it themselves. They depend upon it as much as someone in a wheelchair depends upon the goodness and gentleness of others.

They also walk with a limp (the limp of Jacob). Arrogance is anathema to them, especially when they encounter it in themselves. They know from experience that Brokenness awaits them not too far ahead. When they see it in others, they fear for them, knowing it will bring others to the place of true humility, too—not for punishment's sake, but for mercy's sake, for destiny, for Union's ultimate desire.

It is true that, most of the time, arrogant people do not even realize they are arrogant; they fail to see it in themselves. It is most sad, for it is clear that Brokenness will bring them to difficult decisions, unless, of course, they run from her. Then the arrogant will have untold pain awaiting them.

Yes, no matter how you look at it, Brokenness is always the easier path.

Those who know Brokenness as a lifelong companion often see her coming near to those who need her friendship and love. They will pray that Brokenness has her way with them.

Please don't ask me how I know these things. But, since you have read this far, I am sure you already know.

Arrogance and other roadblocks of life keep us from hearing the Voice of the Lord. If we do manage to hear the Voice, we begin a lifelong journey with Brokenness following us closely. It is true that discernment, intercession, and utterance will be accepted and most effected through vessels that are broken, flowing with His Spirit, and unencumbered by the hindrances of fleshy constraints and religious baggage.

WHAT IS JESUS BUILDING?

Can we rightly ask what He is *not* building? Probably that is a question that every person needs to answer individually. It is certain that He is working His miracle within each of us, but the broader question may be whether or not we are being encouraged by those who are also giving themselves to their Lord each day as we are. When we spend time with others who share our passion for Him, the steadier, more grounded, and more focused our lives seem to be.

I offer these following views for you to examine and meditate on. Maybe you can find yourself living among them somewhere.

OUT OF EGYPT

Metaphorically speaking, let us consider the Fellowship of Egypt. It thrives today much like the bondage of Egypt that the children of Israel had to undergo. The people in this Fellowship are not going anywhere. They are stuck in the prison of their thoughts, their theology. I certainly don't look down on them at all. I feel their pain as if it were mine because, at one time, it was. My heart goes out to them. I want to reach them in love and compassion, just as someone reached out to me in heartfelt love when I needed it most.

However, I must always remember that I cannot reach out to anyone if I am a prisoner of Egypt as well. But the Voice is coming to this Fellowship like He came to me and to so many others over the years—with the Flowing Presence that will set many free. Maybe you will be one of many thousands who will bring the River of the Water of Life to the deserts of this Egypt Fellowship.

THE VOICE FOR ANCIENT ISRAEL

As each day passed, Israel's strength in Egypt faded, as did their hope for deliverance. Little did they know that God was preparing a Voice for them. Little did they understand that their days in the bondage of Egypt were numbered.

Moses was coming, but they did not know it. When he arrived, God's Voice was on the scene and their deliverance was at hand. It did not take much for the million or so Israelites to respond, for it was the Voice of God that they were hearing. It was His Voice that set them free. The Voice from on high moved them forward, out of their bondage.

Once their Deliverer came, they could not and would not want to stay in bondage. Their Deliverer set them absolutely free. The miracles they witnessed and experienced would lead them into a freedom that left their land of bondage as nothing more than a wasteland. They carried its memory into the wilderness, where it would haunt them until the next miraculous Voice would lead them into the Land of Promise.

THE FELLOWSHIP OF THE WILDERNESS

The Fellowship of the Wilderness kept the people searching, arguing, struggling, vying for authority, hungering but never being filled, building their authority centers, and going in circles. This Fellowship kept moving, but it never arrived anywhere. These people must have seen their footprints in the sand and their old fire pits over and over again. Nonetheless, they moved on. They saw the fire of God with great rejoicing and the pillars of smoke were a clear sign to them of God's favor. They enjoyed the miracles of manna and quail and the Rock that followed them with plenty of water for all; but they failed to realize that God, in His infinite love for them, was providing for them and giving His blessing and care to them. It was all because of His love for them, not because of their obedience.

Who heard God's voice and rebelled? It was all of the people whom Moses brought out of Egypt! With whom was God angry for forty years? It was with those people who sinned! Their dead bodies lay in the desert. God vowed that they would never enter His place of rest. Who would never go? Those who did not obey God! We can see that they couldn't go in, because they did not believe (Hebrews 3:16-19 PEB).

TODAY'S WILDERNESS?

Little does the modern-day Fellowship of Egypt understand that their unbelief keeps them from moving where they really want to go, to the city made without hands, whose builder and maker is God. They teach and teach and teach some more. They do not understand that God's ultimate intention was, and still is, to take them and us into the Promised Land, the fullness of His Presence, and Union with Him.

He has not changed. Most believers continue to knock around in the wilderness like steel balls in a pinball machine. They are lighting up the slides and making pretty noises, mesmerized by the miracles, just as Israel was while continuing to circle about in the wilderness.

But as it was then, we never come into Union with Him. We never get beyond Pentecost. Is it fear, unbelief, ignorance, or a combination of all three? Somehow, we believe that what we have is all there is. Don't get me wrong. I love miracles. I experience them daily. I see His glorious hand in my life, my family, and those around me all the time; but there is more. He is drawing us to Himself. He has put a yearning in us that cannot be ignored or satisfied by just seeing miracles.

> *Sacrifice and meal offering You have not desired; my ears You have opened; burnt offering and sin offering You have not required. Then I said, "Behold, I come; in the scroll of the book it is written of me. I delight to do Your will, O my God; Your Law is within my heart"* (Psalms 40:6-8).

But this puts us in the proverbial pickle. We cannot or will not or do not know how to go on, but we, the people, have a yearning to go on. So leaders will do one of several things. They will develop doctrines to try to convince "Israel" that they are indeed in the Promised Land already. They may attempt to assure the flock that the Promised Land is Heaven. So the old phrase "Heaven can wait" comes alive again. Either way, there is no forward movement, as they continue to go around in circles. They may teach that we are in and out of the Promised Land daily, depending on our circumstances. They may even teach that the Promised Land is the realm of the Spirit.

IS ANYONE BUYING WHAT THEY ARE SELLING?

But people are not so easily duped. Oh, they might be, if it were not for the aching they feel in their hearts, and if it were not for the Holy Spirit rising within them, calling to them, and beckoning them to respond to the cry of their hearts.

Just like Peter when he was called by Jesus to walk on water, believers are being called to decide what they should do. Peter ultimately sank. However, Jesus pulled him up. Peter heard Jesus' voice, felt His Presence, and realized he had made the right decision. (He heard the Voice of the Lord and moved forward.)

Remember, without hearing the Voice of the Lord, you cannot possibly move on. You will go around in circles. However, after hearing the Voice of the Lord, you cannot stay. Trust the cry of your heart, and love the cry of your heart. The Church Jesus is building will move forward with the sound of a Voice—His!

Unbelief kept the Israelites wandering in the wilderness for forty years. Finally, the Voice of God's authority could be heard above the ranting of mere fleshy people. It was recognized as God's authority without political prowess, doctrinal correction, or religious intimidation. The Voice of the Lord spoke to people, and they responded by following His direction.

Today, these folk are called rebellious, unstable, uncontrollable. Well, they are ultimately uncontrollable, as well they should be, if the Voice is surely speaking to them and through them. They are not holding on to a system or trying to protect anything. They are simply trying to obey the Voice.

THE REAL BATTLE

This is the Church of the Wilderness. This is where the fleshy side of people comes into direct battle for control. Who will rule? Will the fleshy side of people rule, or will God rule? Who will win the day? Very frequently we find that people will submit to God on a given day, but on the next day, they rise up in personal rebellion. One day people want God to use them and build His Kingdom through them. The next day or the next moment, though, they want recognition, and they rise up to be seen by everyone.

There are times when people want to be hidden. "I must decrease," is the cry of their hearts. They shout, "Let Christ increase!" At the first opportunity, though, they crawl over a brother or sister who has faltered in order to rise above others and be seen by all. "It's by His mercy," they say quietly.

The wilderness is a battleground between flesh and Spirit, soul and Spirit. Will the gifts of the Spirit take precedence? Will the need for cash cause a fleshy reaction to the need of the day? Is my need human-made, or is it God-called? Is my desire God-planted or self-proclaimed? Is my calling a God-calling or a self-indulgent, impatient proclamation? The battle rages on. This classic struggle has been replayed over and over again throughout the ages, and it always ends by determining whether Brokenness has won the day or not.

There was a time when I was certain that God wanted me to start a television program that was aimed specifically at teens. My goal was to eventually broadcast the show all night long in order to reach teens who needed help. I had a great lineup of teen hosts, excellent directors, and a dedicated staff. Indeed, I had everything that was needed for such a show, except for a word from the Lord. This was in the early Nineties. The cost to do it would be close to three quarters of a million dollars by today's dollar—money I did not have. It would also cost me my ego—and there was plenty of that!

Brokenness came very close during that time of my life. Cathy, my awesome wife and dearest friend, stood with me through this time of uncertainty and turmoil. Eventually, I knew I had to stand before my church congregation, my Destiny Image family, and my own family. I repented of my pride and my grandiose plans. My heart was right, but I had missed God by a country mile.

This was not easy for me. My health suffered, as well. My family and my friends forgave me. I have yet to recover my health. I hope I never recover my ego. You'll have to ask Cathy about that part.

A Frightful Place of Warfare and Struggle

Yes, the wilderness is a frightful place of warfare and struggle. It is where a person stands on the precipice of financial windfall or ruin. It could go either way. It is where services are sometimes a cross between Christianity, parlor tricks, and a three-ring circus just to get folk to join in and to keep things going. It's a very tough sell. Most CEOs wouldn't be able to do what most pastors have to do to keep their churches functional.

Organizations that are endeavoring to function in the wilderness are often just treading water in terms of real spiritual growth. We must realize that there has not been true spiritual groundbreaking as a result of forward-moving truth for a century or more. Even the recent revivals and renewals that have taken place in various places around the world were consumed by things that we do not have time to discuss here, although they were certainly well-intentioned. The people involved were hoping for so much more than what was accomplished in the Spirit. Instead of moving forward, we merely revitalized what was done in the past. We allowed the jealousy and arrogance of those with big microphones to direct what God wanted to direct. Therefore, the Voice was silenced.

The anticipation and excitement related to the Voice went away, as did the Spirit of the Lord. Of course, an explanation was offered, "It was time for the revival to end. God had accomplished His work." And so we wait for the next one, or I should say, some are waiting for it. There are those, though, who will respond to God's Voice without the need for a revival. They will simply let the Lord Jesus be who He is. They will risk being called heretics, as the Church fathers of old were called when they ushered in truth that had been lost and was restored at the cost of their reputations and all too frequently their lives as well.

We retrain and disciple each new generation afresh, but we teach them the same old things. This is not necessarily wrong, but it's simply treading water. We find new ways to say old things, and in so doing, we make no progress. The foundations are necessary, but we cannot call them "new" unless they are taking us forward, which they are not. There is no new water, no new wind, no new anything. Fearful of being called heretics, most are afraid even to discuss new thoughts, really groundbreaking revelations that could very well launch the Church Jesus is building into exciting new areas and directions we've only dreamed about.

In all fairness, every believer can respond to God. It isn't just up to the pastor. We are all members of God's priesthood. The River flows from each of us. His Voice leads and encourages every one of us to go forward. God does not want anyone to be camping on yesterday's revelation or yesterday's direction. All of us are responsible for hearing the Voice for ourselves, and responding to what He is saying.

I am certain that on Judgment Day, few leaders will take responsibility for your life, your choices, or your actions, whether good or bad. I am also certain that your excuse for not responding to the Voice will fail if it involves having obeyed your pastor first. This does not mean that you are free to ignore or avoid sound counsel. It does mean that you are responsible for what you know you are hearing, even after you've received counsel from others, prayer, attitude checks, Scripture checks, and more prayer. Yes, you are the responsible party.

Therefore, just as the Holy Spirit says:

> *...The Spirit also helps our weakness; for we do not know how to pray as we should, but the Spirit Himself intercedes for us with groanings too deep for words; and He who searches the hearts knows what the mind of the Spirit is, because He intercedes for the saints according to the will of God* (Romans 8:26-27).

> *Who will condemn? Christ Jesus is the one who died and was raised from death. And, he is at God's right side, talking to God for us* (Romans 8:34 PEB).

> *Joshua said to the sons of Israel, "How long will you put off entering to take possession of the land which the LORD, the God of your fathers, has given you?"* (Joshua 18:3).

Then Joshua commanded the officers of the people, saying, "Pass through the midst of the camp and command the people, saying, 'Prepare provisions for yourselves, for within three days you are to cross this Jordan, to go in to possess the land which the Lord *your God is giving you, to possess it'"* (Joshua 1:10-11).

In the Church Jesus is building, His Voice is heard in the worship, in children's school, from the podium, everywhere! The witness is everywhere. God's Voice speaks in the Sunday school, adult Bible study, the choir, meetings of the board, and even at church gatherings such as picnics.

Listen for the Voice and respond to it with all your heart.

Freedom

I wonder why so many believers love the movie *Braveheart*. Many people on Facebook list it as one of their all-time favorites. In worship services, one often hears the cry of "Freedom!" shouted as it was at the end of this movie. Maybe it is because deep within the human heart, people know that they are bound. They are looking for freedom from their bondage. They know they are unable to do what their hearts tell them to do. Most believers know that they cannot fulfill their destinies as they are positioned now.

The Church Jesus is building releases believers to become what they have always known in their hearts that they should be. Theirs is a cry that cannot be silenced. It is clear that from the bottom up, from leaders to the ones they are serving, there needs to be a single, driving passion to see everyone free so that Jesus can become one with them. Pastors should be leading their flocks to green pastures and cool springs of water. It is there that Jesus will meet them and do His work within them. The most exciting destiny that ignites the heart of a believer is to see Jesus flowing from a believer whose life used to be characterized by despair and heartache.

No one should ever fear freedom, for it is the yearning of every heart to be free. Free believers truly change their lives and the world around them.

TRUTH

Pilate said to Him, "So You are a king?" Jesus answered, "You say correctly that I am a king. For this I have been born, and for this I have come into the world, to testify to the truth. Everyone who is of the truth hears My voice." Pilate said to Him, "What is truth?" And when he had said this, he went out again to the Jews and said to them, "I find no guilt in Him" (John 18:37-38).

And the Word became flesh, and dwelt among us, and we saw His glory, glory as of the only begotten from the Father, full of grace and truth (John 1:14).

The Law was given through Moses; grace and truth were realized through Jesus Christ (John 1:17).

Jesus said to him, "I am the way, and the truth, and the life; no one comes to the Father but through Me" (John 14:6).

Truth is a person. He lives. Pilate posed a question that he thought was deep and philosophical: "What is truth?" It came from his frustration to be sure, but he didn't understand that he was talking to the answer! Had he waited for an answer, maybe Jesus would have told him.

This same question has frustrated people throughout the centuries. As I was talking to Cathy about this, she went into one of her usually awesome mini-talks, and I began to take notes. Her points kept on speaking to me for a time after that. In fact, her ideas have formed the basis for this part of the book. (Thank you, Cathy.)

If Jesus is truth, why were so few words written about Him during His three years of ministry? Why didn't He write scrolls or spend more time just teaching His disciples?

Jesus *is* truth. He is actually more than truth. He is the journey through truth, the exploration about truth, and the discovery of truth. The physical man Christ Jesus was the only part of Him that was visible in the time-and-space dimension. His physical appearance, however, was only the tip of the iceberg. All of eternity cannot contain all the truth that Jesus is. Therefore, to say that all the truth that He embodies is actually contained in the four Gospels is utterly absurd. Our mighty, multidimensional God cannot be contained, understood, or limited to the brains of mere mortals, even if they are disciples of the Lord Himself. We are not equal with God, and to think we can completely fathom the truth that Jesus is would diminish His power and authority.

We must understand these things before we can move on. One of the reasons there are so many denominations, and why so many do not believe in ongoing revelation, is because there is such a limited understanding of the truth that Jesus is. Too many people believe that what God spoke to their leaders in past generations is enough revelation for them. They believe there can be no further revelation.

Though they are sincere, they are sincerely locked into a system of belief that keeps them from hearing from God. This in turn keeps them from growing and learning the new things God has in store for them.

As I mentioned before, we live in an Amish area of southeastern Pennsylvania. The Amish heard the Lord telling them to separate themselves from worldly lifestyles many generations ago. They obeyed the Voice, and this kept them and their children from being led astray. Over the years, though, this word has locked them into a legalism that has turned their communities into a sect that has, in some cases, actually become a cult. They reject any probability that God can speak anything new to them. They are caught up in their old lifestyle—a lifestyle that keeps them from experiencing the freedom God wants them to have.

Journey Through Time

The Voice of the Lord thunders: "Truth is not like math. Truth is a journey. It develops. Because of this, many are afraid to write, since what they have written one year will appear to be wrong a few years later."

The books and articles we write and the talks we give serve to chronicle our journey through time. They are important markers to have. They are our history. They will show future generations how our thoughts, revelation, and growth developed over time. I personally love to read the works I've written in times past. I can see how my Christian walk has developed as I have gotten older. It is an important measure that shows me that I have been open to the Holy Spirit and He has been able to instruct me.

Jesus (Truth) leads us on. He doesn't change, but we do. He redefines us, clarifies who we are, and changes our minds constantly.

Truth is alive, vibrant, exciting. I get up in the morning and cannot wait to see what new things Jesus will challenge me with that day.

Am I fickle? Are my beliefs so random that mere whims passing my spirit change my whole system of belief? There are many who would like to believe that. Actually, there are many who do believe that, and they use it against me all the time. Folk who fear for their own theology and systems of belief are unable to imagine Truth beyond ink on paper. That is the easy way out, to be sure. All true relationships are dynamic, evolving, changing, so is our relationship with the one we marry.

On our wedding day, we know so little about the person we are marrying. Nonetheless, our unity is the beginning, not the culmination of our journey together. Why then do we think that our Union with God is written in stone? Cathy and I have been married a long time. Even so, I am discovering new things about her every day, and she is learning new things about me. Our marriage—our oneness—is a lifetime of discovery. We are finite beings, yet our depth cannot be discovered in a lifetime. How much more must this be true of our relationship with the Lord?

When we believe that Truth (Jesus) can be learned like a course in mathematics, we are finished. Truth is a unique spiritual experience that supernaturally changes a human being into a new species, a new creation. Truth miraculously merges the natural with the spiritual, creating a Union of which Jesus is the firstborn of many brethren.

> *If anyone is in Christ, he is a new creature; the old things passed away; behold, new things have come* (2 Corinthians 5:17).

It doesn't matter whether a person is circumcised or uncircumcised. All that is important is being a new creation (Galatians 6:15 PEB).

He rescued us from the domain of darkness, and transferred us to the kingdom of His beloved Son, in whom we have redemption, the forgiveness of sins. He is the image of the invisible God, the firstborn of all creation (Colossians 1:13-15).

SHOW THE JOURNEY

Truth (Jesus) continuously marinates us and breaks us so that the flavor of Christ—all that He is—can flow through us as naturally as our breath. Christ never changes, but our perception of whom He is changes constantly. The danger is stopping at one perception of Him, naming it, and staying there. It takes humility to admit that a perception of Him is just that—a perception, an understanding of who He is at a given point in time.

At Destiny Image, we often have authors who want to change a book every time it goes for a reprint. They want to update their changing perceptions. That, however, is unfair to the readers. Believers need to see the journey as it unfolds. They need to see that it is not only OK to change, but that it is a normal part of the believer's life. It is the main indicator that they actually have a living and dynamic relationship with their Lord.

Books are the road maps that reveal where we have been and where we are headed as we sojourn through time. It was never intended that we should take only baby steps through time as our theological overseers saw fit. A close study of history reveals that it was the renegades and revolutionaries who dared to buck the tide of established systems and thereby enabled believers to go deeper into the purposes of God.

It was never the established leader or the status quo that led the folk into something new. As soon as leaders regained the upper hand, religion returned to its corrupt stagnating system of mind control and people control.

The Church Jesus is building, on the other hand, will be led by Him continuously. In His Church, the River of the Water of Life will flow freely, powerfully, and without interruption. It will cut the way into new perceptions, new revelations, and new levels of love and compassion. If our approaches do not lead to the greater genuine visibility of Christ in our lives, we are simply wasting our time going down wrong pathways. Brokenness will have to humble us, open us to the needs of all humankind, as we learn to become true gatherers. That's what Jesus demonstrated for us again and again.

> *When He* [Jesus] *went ashore, He saw a large crowd, and felt compassion for them and healed their sick. When it was evening, the disciples came to Him and said, "This place is desolate and the hour is already late; so send the crowds away, that they may go into the villages and buy food for themselves." But Jesus said to them, "They do not need to go away; you give them something to eat!"* (Matthew 14:14-16).

> *Then Peter came and said to Him, "Lord, how often shall my brother sin against me and I forgive him? Up to seven times?" Jesus said to him, "I do not say to you, up to seven times, but up to seventy times seven"* (Matthew 18:21-22).

Then some children were brought to Him so that He might lay His hands on them and pray; and the disciples rebuked them. But Jesus said, "Let the children alone, and do not hinder them from coming to Me; for the kingdom of heaven belongs to such as these." After laying His hands on them, He departed from there (Matthew 19:13-15).

The Church Jesus is building does not separate; it gathers. It does not condemn; it loves and leaves the judgment to God, the Father of all. The River of God is within. Remember that it flows forward. If we do not resist, the same River will carry us forward as well.

LET THE RIVER FLOW

The turnaround of our country and our world is contingent upon the Voice. The Voice is contingent upon the River of the Water of Life flowing from the Throne of God, which is within you and me.

It is impossible for human beings to change nations or the world in their own power. However, when the River is flowing and men and women yield to the River and the Voice, the task of changing the world around us becomes much easier. The River is the Presence of God, and God's will is to establish His Kingdom within the hearts of all of us.

Our inabilities and limitations do not mean that we should ignore the heartbreaking scenes in our neighborhoods and the world. The love of God has always had one focus: the total redemption of humankind. The resurrection of the Lord Jesus Christ assured believers that His redemption and the flow of His Life would be effective and continuous. The Voice keeps on thundering life, healing, love, direction, compassion, and wholeness in ways that we will never completely understand.

Those who are carrying His Voice throughout the Earth have come to know Him in deep and abiding ways. They yearn for His Life, love His Presence, weep over His giving nature, and feed on His mercy. No longer will they be satisfied with simply being His messengers. They want to know Him personally and experience Him as friend, brother, Lord, and King. They have become ecstatic to realize that this was His plan all along.

The Lord wasn't looking for messengers; the angels could do that. He wanted people with whom He could experience a true Union that would affect them in every way—body, soul, and spirit. He wanted the kind of relationship that would marry power with character, spirituality, and Brokenness. It would also wed holiness of outward expression with devotion. This leads to inner peace with God. It is the kind of testimony able to convince the world that the light shining in the darkness truly comes from the heart of the inner person. The inner Christ demonstrates that the simple believer, filled with the Voice, is the genuine article.

This is the normal believer's life. It cannot be learned in Bible school. In this kind of relationship, the Scriptures are etched on the believer's heart, not simply memorized by the believer's brain. The Word of God is melded into the spirit of the person so that one cannot discern where the person ends and the Spirit begins, because Union has blurred the line between the two.

As you can tell, this has become the passion of my heart. All that matters is the blurring of the line between human and God for all believers, for all humankind.

God wants His Voice to be heard. He knows that when His Voice is spoken, it will be heard. When His Voice is heard, all creation hears and responds.

WE ARE HIS

What do we truly have to offer the Lord for His service to us? We can offer ourselves to Him. We are His Throne. Humanity is the source of the Earth's supply because we are the convergence of two dimensions—the natural and the spiritual. Eternity and time/space come together in us. Our hearts are the Most Holy Place within which the Presence dwells. The River flows there. The Voice emanates and resonates from there.

Think for a moment of what God accomplished by sending Jesus to Earth. God flowed through Him.

> *Those whom He foreknew, He also predestined to become conformed to the image of His Son, so that He would be the firstborn among many brethren...* (Romans 8:29).

> *By this, love is perfected with us, so that we may have confidence in the day of judgment; because as He is, so also are we in this world* (1 John 4:17).

VOICE-TO-VOICE EXPERIENCE

When I was a child, I loved God so much that it made my heart ache. I didn't know how to describe my feelings with words back then, but now I know and understand what was happening to me.

Sometimes I went to church several times a week. I was looking for something that would make me feel even closer to God than I did. It seemed that the aching in my heart was unbearable at times.

I began to take the booklets from the church to read at home, thinking that this would help me somehow. These booklets contained prayers and devotions that were written by men who were bishops in the church. It was very exciting to me. I was sure the booklets would help me. However, they did not help, and I grew even more frustrated.

Then I found devotions that were written by a man who did not sign his name. These anonymous devotions seemed to be different from the other booklets I had read. They caused my heart to leap within me. I felt I was on fire with the love of God. I read and read and read. "Who is this guy?" I wondered. "I would love to meet him."

Years later, when I got my first Bible from the cute young lady who would become my wife, I found some markings in the Book of Psalms. It was then that I realized who had written these devotionals. It was none other than King David! The Voice in David had stirred the Voice in me long before I ever prayed the Sinner's Prayer. Ha! The River was gushing through me long before traditional Western doctrine said it could.

Later, when pastors would tell me that the Church was in the wilderness, but that Jesus comes to live in our hearts, I just didn't get it. Matter of fact, I still don't get it. How can we be in the wilderness with Jesus living in our hearts? We can't have it both ways, can we? The New Covenant teachings of Jesus say that we are complete in Him. How can the River of Life flow through me in the wilderness? This just doesn't make sense to me at all.

THE BLOOD OF JESUS COVERS US— HIS POWER DELIVERS US

What do these things have to do with the Voice? Everything. If we live in the wilderness, we spend our lives worrying about whether or not our salvation is secure, just as the children of Israel worried about their food and water for the day. They worried daily, realizing that the next day they would worry again. If we must struggle for our salvation or our day-to-day sustenance, little else will matter to us. In fact, we won't have time for anything else. Earning and keeping our salvation would be our full-time concern.

All of this changes when we really understand that we have been bought with a price. Everything changes when we understand that we have been prepared by our Creator for a Union that causes the River of His Life to flow freely through us, bringing to us everything we need and more. Do we lose our salvation every time we sin? If the River runs through us, does He reroute the River every time we screw up? Really? I doubt it.

Therefore, we can have a clear focus about these important matters. Our focus should be upon yielding to Him within, not on whether I am saved today or tomorrow. The Blood of Jesus covers us until His power delivers us from life's situations.

I wonder why believers so frequently teach and live by the examples of Israel in the wilderness. I simply don't understand that focus at all. We are not in the wilderness anymore. We sing about the wilderness, many teach as though we were still there, and so many live, suffer, and die as if the wilderness were their home.

The New Covenant was initiated within the Veil. We are, in fact, in the Promised Land now. We don't have to beg God, decree, pronounce, renounce, announce, or pounce on anything. We are the children of God. The fleshy, self-absorbed antics of childhood have passed away. We say we are mature. If we are, then our maturity should be evident in our love, gentleness, humility, mercy, compassion, forgiveness, generosity, kindness, and gathering nature. It is time to throw away our deceitful, hateful, childish pranks. Let us examine all our treasured, fleshy, childish toys and put them out at someone else's religious yard sale.

BLESSED UNION

Union with God makes everything that is His, ours. But it also makes everything that is ours, His. We love the first sentence, but we struggle with the second. We really do want all that is His, but we only want to give Him 10 percent of what is ours.

What a deal this is for us! Our yieldedness has to be mutual. We easily accept that He gave all for us. We, in turn, must give our all to Him. Our Union with Him is as real as it gets. Maturity brings us to the inevitable conclusion that we are working as one, for we truly are one.

The words of Jesus begin to make much more sense as time goes on. He said:

> *In that day you will know that I am in My Father,*
> *and you in Me, and I in you* (John 14:20).

> *I am the vine, you are the branches; he who abides*
> *in Me and I in him, he bears much fruit, for apart*
> *from Me you can do nothing* (John 15:5).

Our Union with God is so profound that everything concerning us becomes completely brand-new. In the Book of Galatians, Paul stresses this by saying that even though he was a Jew, his Jewishness did not matter in comparison to his being a new creation in Christ: *"It doesn't matter whether a person is circumcised or uncircumcised. All that is important is being a new creation"* (Galatians 6:15 PEB).

As we read the Gospel of John, it becomes clear that the purpose of the Cross was to purify us, not for Heaven, but for Union with God, so He would become the Voice in the Earth. The Voice would be articulated through the new creation—the Voice that would roar from the River of the Water of Life, flowing from His Throne within the human heart.

THE VOICE IS CONVINCING

There are believers who are hearing the Lord's Voice deep within their hearts. His Voice is convincing them. It's time for them to move beyond their comfort zone into new territory. There may be only a few who are hearing His Voice, but these are the ones who are willing to go where God is leading them. A true heart of broken humility is always the key. Anger, pride, condescension, and arrogance will block His Voice and make it more difficult for others to see God at work in them. If God is calling, there is no need to demonstrate anything but quiet confidence.

Wait upon the Lord, move forward with hopeful expectancy. Respectfully listen, wait, evaluate, and pray. The decision is yours. It is impossible to want the freedom of making your own decisions in God without taking responsibility for the results of those decisions. Too many take the coward's way out by blaming everyone but themselves. There is absolutely no growth for the one who engages in blame-shifting. I've heard folk blame their pastor, their spouse, their prayer partner, a television evangelist, and others. Some even blame God for purposely leading them in a certain direction and then abandoning them. How absurd this is! The responsibility is yours!

I have known some people who ended up needing counseling because they were offended at God for "leading" them to start a business and then "abandoning" them. All I can say is, "That was not God."

FOLLOW THE LEAD OR FOLLOW THE LEADER?

The Voice remains convincing, however. When a person is not genuinely convinced to take a leap of faith, he or she probably has not heard the Voice at all. I have a theory that is perhaps more fact-based than most will want to admit. The Voice is rather easy to hear. Therefore, the Voice is not the problem. It is obedience to the Voice that most people struggle with. It is easier to say that we are confused or that we can't hear His Voice or that God never speaks to us. Perhaps we think that if we can convince everyone of our inability to hear God, we will be free from whatever He is calling us to do.

I am here to tell you that it does not work that way. If we do not hear God, or if we are unsure whether we are hearing Him, it seems safe to follow others who say they are hearing His Voice. This has the effect of freeing us from the responsibility of listening and deciding for ourselves. This causes us to follow the leader instead of following the lead given by the Voice.

It is easy to hide within ourselves, because no one really knows that we are doing so. No one sees what we are doing. However, others may wonder why we are not growing as we should be. Certainly we are accepted as we are, but we soon realize that we are falling behind, and the danger arises that we might be left behind altogether. These are the natural results of not hearing and moving with the Voice of the Lord.

A few years ago, Cathy wanted me to start a diet. You know what that's like. A diet is an endless no-win attempt to lose what you don't want. Being overweight is a constant challenge, but a diet may not help all that much. The weight eventually finds you again and crawls back on you while you sleep at night! Or at least is seems to.

Nonetheless, I agreed to try another diet. It was just like every other diet I had ever tried. Cathy fixed the perfect breakfast, and I would sneak the perfect snack. She fixed a good lunch, and I would seek a good snack. It was a perfect system, and I never got caught until the Lord nailed me!

He began to show me what I was doing. It might seem funny, but it wasn't clear to me until I saw it. I continued to put on weight, even though Cathy didn't see everything I ate. Then I realized it was not between me and her at all; it was between me and my body. It was simple: *I* ate and *I* gained weight.

The same thing is true with hearing the Voice. We may say that we are confused or that we can't hear His Voice. We may even go so far as to say, "God never speaks to me." We must realize, however, that this is not between the pastor and us and not between our friends and us. It is between us and the Lord. We may be able to fool others, but we can never fool Him.

Sometimes we even fool ourselves into thinking that we will be the Voice. How can we be the Voice if we never hear the Voice? The Union between people and their Creator is not just a feel-good experience. Neither is the union between a man and a woman always a feel-good experience. However, if we find this Union with God, it will blossom into an eternity of inexplicable love, beauty, growth, strength, and fulfillment.

This will be characteristic of every believer who is a part of the Church Jesus is building. It begins with Brokenness and humility and then is carried by the River of the Water of Life into a new realm of fruitfulness that stems from our Union with God. That Union enables us to hear the Voice and respond to it with loving obedience.

This is what God wants for you and me, and nothing in life can be more important than this.

Oswald Chambers wrote:

> God has ventured all in Jesus Christ to save us, now He wants us to venture out all in abandoned confidence in Him. There are spots where that faith has not worked in us as yet, places untouched by the life of God. There were none of those spots in Jesus Christ's life, and there are to be none in ours. "This is life eternal, that they might know Thee." The real meaning of eternal life is a life that can face anything it has to face without wavering. If we take this view, life becomes one great romance, a glorious opportunity for seeing marvelous things all the time. God is disciplining us to get us into this central place of power.[1]

I hear the Voice calling. You do, too. I know because I know you. Your spirit leaped as you read this book just as mine did as I wrote it. You will be all right. I am sure of it. I know your heart.

ENDNOTE

1. Oswald Chambers, *My Utmost for His Highest*, quoted in *God's Treasury of Virtues* (Tulsa, OK: Honor Books, 1995), 170.

ABOUT DON NORI SR.

Don Nori Sr., Founder of Destiny Image Publishers, has worked in the publishing industry and ministered internationally for more than thirty years, working with people of all races and nationalities. Don and his wife, Cathy, live at the foot of the Appalachian Mountains in south central Pennsylvania where they raised their five sons and now enjoy their daughters-in-law and their grandchildren. Don spends most of his time writing and ministering internationally.

Visit Don Nori's website for his itinerary, video blogs, and new books: www.donnorisr.com.

You may also view his YouTube videos at www.youtube.com/donnorisr, as well as viewing his daily posts and interacting with him on Facebook: https://www.facebook.com/donald.nori.

To contact him regarding a speaking engagement, e-mail him at: donnorisr@gmail.com

In the right hands, This Book will Change Lives!

Most of the people who need this message will not be looking for this book. To change their lives, you need to put a copy of this book in their hands.

> *But others (seeds) fell into good ground, and brought forth fruit, some a hundred-fold, some sixty-fold, some thirty-fold* (Matthew 13:8).

Our ministry is constantly seeking methods to find the good ground, the people who need this anointed message to change their lives. Will you help us reach these people?

> *Remember this—a farmer who plants only a few seeds will get a small crop. But the one who plants generously will get a generous crop* (2 Corinthians 9:6).

EXTEND THIS MINISTRY BY SOWING
3 BOOKS, 5 BOOKS, 10 BOOKS, OR MORE TODAY,
AND BECOME A LIFE CHANGER!

Thank you,

Don Nori Sr., Founder
Destiny Image
Since 1982

DESTINY IMAGE PUBLISHERS, INC.

"Promoting Inspired Lives."

VISIT OUR NEW SITE HOME AT
WWW.DESTINYIMAGE.COM

FREE SUBSCRIPTION TO DI NEWSLETTER

Receive free unpublished articles by top DI authors, exclusive
discounts, and free downloads from our best and newest books.
Visit www.destinyimage.com to subscribe.

Write to: Destiny Image
             P.O. Box 310
             Shippensburg, PA 17257-0310

Call: 1-800-722-6774

Email: orders@destinyimage.com

For a complete list of our titles or to place an order
online, visit www.destinyimage.com.

FIND US ON FACEBOOK OR FOLLOW US ON TWITTER.

www.facebook.com/destinyimage   facebook
www.twitter.com/destinyimage   twitter